INTRODUCTION TO APPLE WRITER WORD PROCESSING

H. JAMES WATTS

JAMES F. CLARK
Fulton County Schools
Atlanta, Georgia

W77

Published by
SOUTH-WESTERN PUBLISHING CO.

CINCINNATI   WEST CHICAGO, IL   DALLAS   PELHAM MANOR, NY   PALO ALTO, CA

ISBN: 0-538-23770-8

Library of Congress Catalog Card Number: 83-50531

4 5 6 7 8 9 10 K 7 6 5

Printed in the United States of America

Preface

Word processing has become an important tool for improving office productivity. For those seeking employment, the ability to operate a word processor opens many doors. For the professional whose work involves writing, word processing skills greatly increase the efficiency of composition and revision.

This text teaches *Apple Writer*®[1] word processing. More importantly, however, it teaches general word processing concepts that can be applied to any other system with which the user may be confronted. Lessons emphasize the format and purpose of various business documents, along with the word processing functions to be used in creating the documents.

Each lesson includes a written exercise. This exercise helps develop a clearer understanding of the material presented in the lesson. Once each lesson is studied and the written exercise is completed, a computer application problem provides hands-on experience.

A glossary contains all new vocabulary words presented in the text, as well as the basic control characters. This makes quick reference and review much easier.

This text may be used with *Apple Writer*® II software on the Apple® II, Apple® II Plus, or Apple® IIe microcomputer. All instructions, illustrations, and examples in the text are given for the Apple II or Apple II Plus. If *Apple Writer* II is being used on the Apple IIe, there is one primary difference to keep in mind. The keyboard of the Apple IIe contains additional keys that do not appear on an Apple II or an Apple II Plus. Any significant changes in procedure that this difference may cause are described in this text.

Written in a straightforward, easy-to-understand manner, this text is designed to be self-teaching. Mastery of the material, whether done for vocational or personal reasons, is a valuable and rewarding accomplishment.

---

[1]Apple® II, Apple® II Plus, Apple® IIe, Apple Writer®, and Apple Writer® II are registered trademarks of Apple Computer, Inc. Any reference to Apple II, Apple II Plus, Apple IIe, Apple Writer, or Apple Writer II refers to this footnote.

Contents

1. Getting Started with *Apple Writer*

OBJECTIVES:

1. Define word processing.
2. Describe the parts of the Apple computer system.
3. Describe the procedures for the care of diskettes.
4. Define *Apple Writer*.
5. Power up and power down the computer using *Apple Writer*.

You are about to begin an exciting adventure as you learn how to do word processing using *Apple Writer*. This lesson will introduce you to word processing, the Apple computer, and *Apple Writer*.

WHAT IS WORD PROCESSING?

In the past, word processing meant putting thoughts on paper by using a pen, a pencil, or a typewriter. Frequently a person dictated messages to a secretary who wrote them in shorthand before typing them on a typewriter. Then the **document** (information on paper) was sent to the person who was to read it.

Today word processing means using a computer to process **text** (groups of words) and produce documents. These documents can be memorandums, letters, reports, or even books. The contents of the document may be dictated to a person who enters them into a computer, or they may be entered into a computer by the person who composes them. Words are entered into the computer by means of a keyboard. As the words are entered, they appear on a television screen. This screen is known as a CRT (an abbreviation for cathode-ray tube) or monitor. If a keying error is made, it is very easily corrected. Likewise, words or sentences can be added or deleted without rekeying correct copy.

When the text entered into the computer is correct, it may be saved or recorded for future use. Also, it can be printed in the form of a document. In order to make changes or corrections in the document, the text can be recalled from storage and the desired changes can be made. It is not necessary to reenter the entire document. The changed document can then be printed. Some computers used for word processing also have the ability to electronically send a message to a computer at another location rather than producing a paper copy for delivery by messenger or mail.

INTRODUCTION TO THE APPLE COMPUTER

The computer system you will be using for word processing is an Apple II or an Apple IIe. The parts of the computer system, shown in Figure 1.1, are connected with cables. The following paragraphs describe the parts of the Apple computer system.

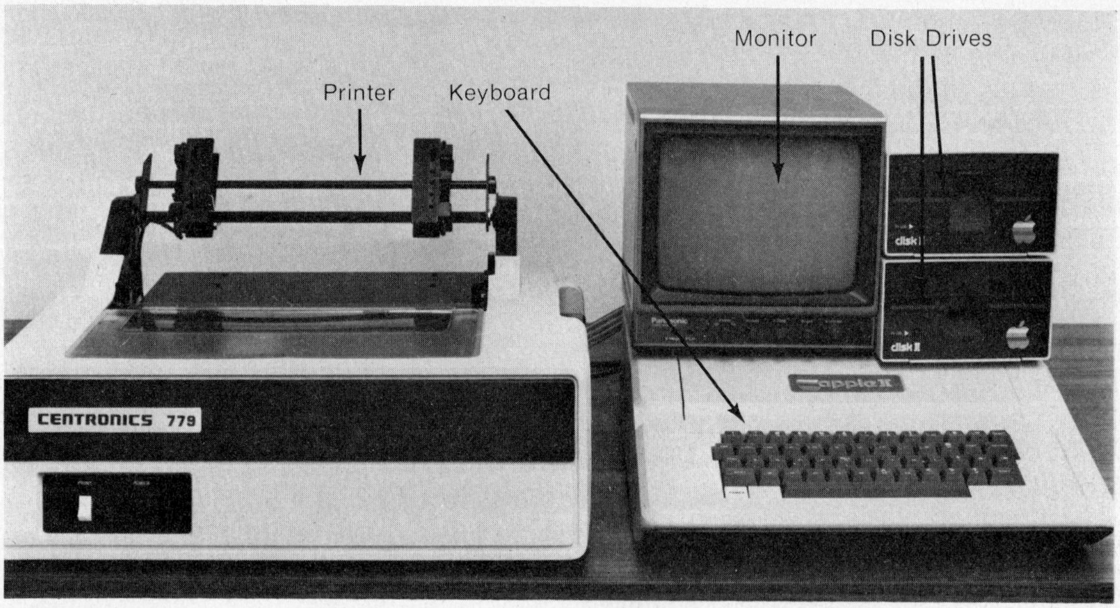

Figure 1.1 Parts of the Apple Computer System

Keyboard

The keyboard of the Apple computer is similar to that of a typewriter. It is used to key the text that is being entered into the computer. There are several keys on the Apple computer keyboard that are not on a typewriter keyboard or are used differently. These will be explained when you first need to use them.

Monitor

The monitor, also known as a CRT, is a television screen. The words you enter on the keyboard are displayed on the monitor instead of being printed on paper as they would be with a typewriter. The monitor also displays messages from *Apple Writer* to you.

Disk Drive

The disk drive is a small box attached to the computer by a cable. It is the device that records or saves text entered into the computer. Your computer may have more than one disk drive. A **diskette** (a device similar in appearance to a stereo record) is placed in the disk drive. The surface of the diskette is coated with a magnetic material similar to that on a cassette tape. As the diskette is rotated inside the disk drive, text is magnetically recorded on it. Then, when desired, the text can be read or played back. The diskette is also referred to as a disk or a floppy disk.

Printer

The printer is similar to a typewriter without a keyboard. It can print a document after the text has been entered into the computer. The printer prints a document much faster than a typewriter can. Since the printer is under the control of the computer, no errors are made during the printing. Of course, if you did not correct keying errors while entering the text, those errors will be printed.

CARE OF DISKETTES

The diskettes used with your computer are fragile. Therefore, read and follow these instructions to properly care for each of your diskettes.

1. Do not bend or fold the diskette. Use only a soft-tip pen to write on the diskette label.
2. Keep the diskette away from magnets and magnetic fields. The text stored on the diskette can be erased by magnetic fields.
3. Do not touch the exposed areas of the diskette. Fingerprints can make the diskette unreadable by the computer.
4. Do not expose the diskette to extremely hot or cold temperatures. If the temperature is too hot (such as in a closed car on a hot day), it will melt. If the temperature is too cold, it will become brittle and break.
5. Insert the diskette into the disk drive carefully. Don't force the diskette or the disk drive door. If the door does not close easily, remove the diskette and repeat the process.
6. Replace the diskette in its protective envelope after each use.

GETTING STARTED WITH *APPLE WRITER*

The following paragraphs will describe *Apple Writer* and some changes which may have been made to your computer.

What Is *Apple Writer*?

Apple Writer is a **computer program**, or a group of instructions that makes the computer behave as a word processor. These instructions are prerecorded on the *Apple Writer* diskette and are ready for you to use. The program instructs the computer to allow you to enter text, change text, save text, and print documents.

Computer Changes That Affect *Apple Writer*

If you are using an Apple IIe, you may skip this section. If you are using an Apple II, there are three changes that may have been made to your computer which will affect your use of *Apple Writer*.

80-COLUMN CARD. The standard Apple II computer displays 40 characters on each line of the screen. A **character** is any letter, number, symbol, or space that can be keyed on the keyboard. Your computer may have an 80-column card installed that causes it to display 80 characters on each line of the screen.

LOWERCASE DISPLAY. Your computer may have been changed so that it can display lowercase letters on the screen as well as the standard uppercase letters of the Apple II. This change may have been made by an 80-column card or by some other method.

SHIFT KEY ADAPTER. When using *Apple Writer* with a standard Apple II computer, you use the ESC (escape) key to capitalize letters in your documents. If a shift key adapter has been installed in your computer, however, you will be able to make capital letters with the shift key.

Ask your instructor if any of these changes have been made to your computer. Once you know whether the changes have been made, you are ready to use *Apple Writer*.

Powering Up the Computer

Powering up the computer refers to the process of turning on the different pieces of equipment. When using *Apple Writer*, power up your computer as follows:

1. Turn on the monitor. The location of the power switch will vary depending on the brand of monitor you are using.
2. Insert an *Apple Writer* diskette into the disk drive. If there is more than one disk drive attached to your com-

puter, insert the diskette into Drive 1. If there are no numbers on the drives, ask your instructor which drive to use. Refer to Figure 1.2 and follow these steps for inserting the diskette:

   a. Open the door of the disk drive by gently pulling it up.

   b. Turn the diskette so that the label faces up and the write protect notch (small square cutout) is on the left.

   c. Gently push the diskette all the way into the open slot of the disk drive. If it is hard to push in, remove it and try again. Never force the diskette into the disk drive. Never remove the diskette while the red light on the disk drive is on.

   d. Close the door of the disk drive. If it does not close easily, remove the diskette and insert it again. Do not force the door closed.

3. Turn on the computer. The power switch is located at the left rear of the computer cabinet. When the power is turned on, the disk drive will run briefly. Then a message will appear on the screen. This completes the powering up process.

Figure 1.2 Inserting a Diskette into the Disk Drive

Loading *Apple Writer*

As a part of the powering up process, the *Apple Writer* program is automatically loaded (read or played back) into the computer. The message that appears on the screen at the end of the powering up process is displayed there by the *Apple Writer* program. It is known as a prompt. A **prompt** is a message to you from a computer program telling you what to do next. If your computer does not have an 80-column card, the message will be in the form of a question that says *Do you have lowercase display (Y/N)?* If your computer has been changed so that it can display lowercase letters, strike the Y key for yes. Otherwise, strike the N key for no. Then press the RETURN key. If your computer has an 80-column card installed, this question will be skipped.

Next, the computer will display a prompt that reads *Press RETURN to begin:* Respond to this prompt by pressing the RETURN key. Once you have pressed the RETURN key, a display labeled *Frequently Used Control Characters* will appear on the CRT. This display, which is known as the Editor Menu, is shown in Figure 1.3.

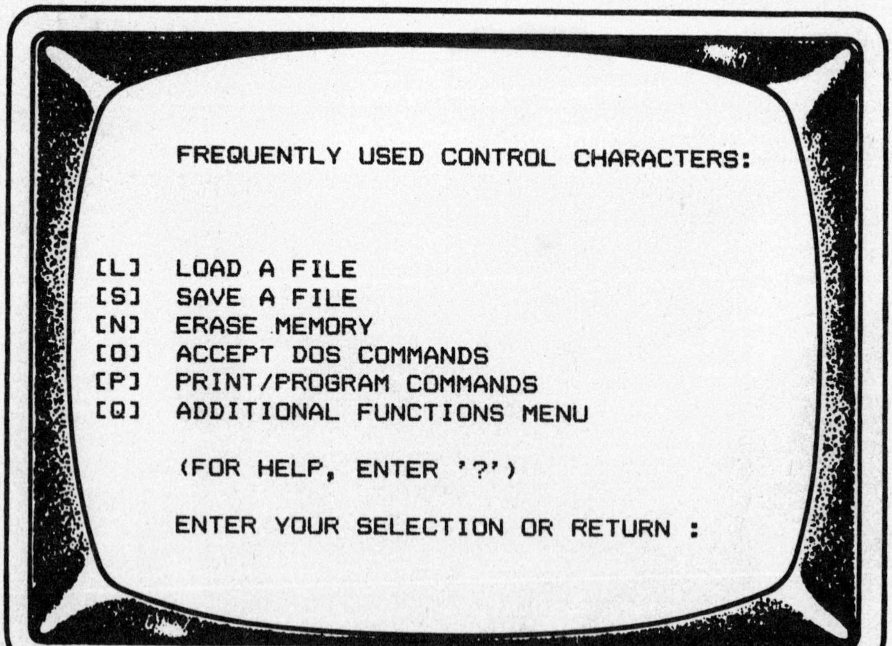

Figure 1.3 *Apple Writer* Editor Menu

Inserting the Student Diskette

Text that you enter into the computer should be stored on a student diskette rather than on the *Apple Writer* diskette. Therefore, when the Editor Menu is first displayed on the screen, you should insert a student diskette. If your computer has one disk drive, gently open the door of the disk drive. Then carefully remove the *Apple Writer* diskette and place it in its protective envelope. Insert your student diskette into the disk drive and carefully close the door. If your computer has two disk drives, you may insert the student diskette into Drive 2 and leave the *Apple Writer* diskette in Drive 1 instead of changing diskettes. (Note: Your instructor may supply you with a ready-to-use student diskette or a new diskette. If a new diskette is supplied, it must be initialized before it is used. The way to do this is explained in the Computer Exercise section of this lesson.)

At this point, you would normally choose to enter text, change text, or print a document. For this first lesson, however, you will just learn how to quit *Apple Writer* and power down the computer.

Quitting *Apple Writer*

When you have finished using *Apple Writer*, you should tell the computer you have finished. This is done by holding down the CTRL (control) key on the left side of the keyboard while striking the Q key. Striking these two keys causes a display known as the Additional Functions Menu to appear on the CRT. The Additional Functions Menu is shown in Figure 1.4.

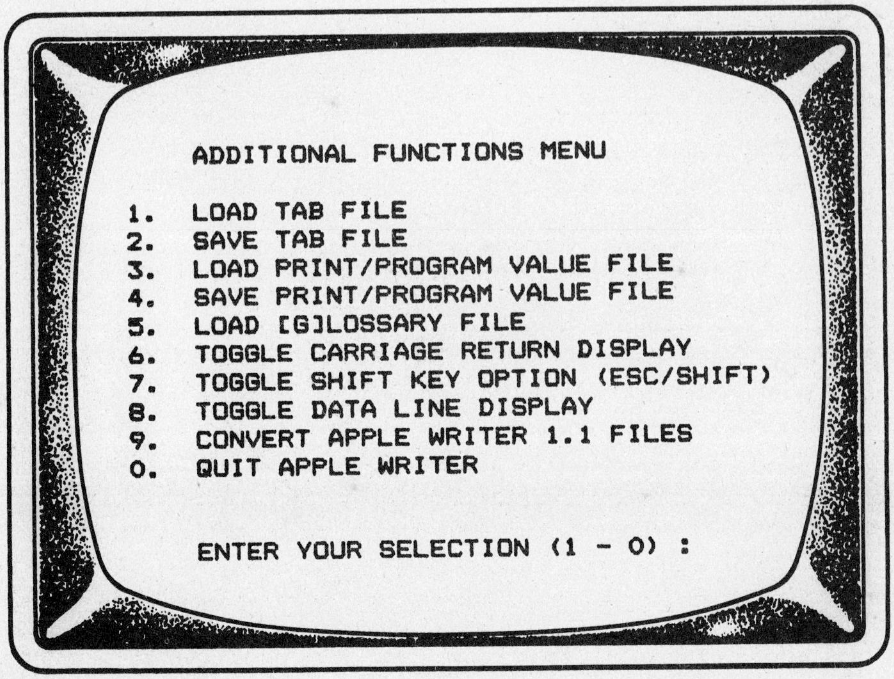

Figure 1.4 Additional Functions Menu

Option 0 of this menu reads *0. Quit Apple Writer.* When you strike the 0 (zero) key, the following message appears on the screen: *Erases Memory. Quit (Y/N)?* Later on you will want to make sure you have saved any entered text before quitting *Apple Writer.* Since you have not entered any text in this first lesson, it is safe to go ahead and strike the Y key. Then press the RETURN key. Remove the diskettes from the disk drives and place them in their protective envelopes.

Powering Down the Computer

As soon as you have removed the diskettes from the disk drives, you may turn off the computer and the monitor. This is known as **powering down** the computer. It does not matter which unit you turn off first.

LESSON 1 EXERCISE Name ______________________ Date __________

Throughout the Exercises, the number of a learning objective appears in parentheses at the end of each question. This number tells you the learning objective in that lesson to which the question corresponds.

TRUE/FALSE

Each of the following statements is either true or false. Indicate your choice in the Answers column by circling T for a true statement or F for a false statement.

		Answers		
1.	Word processing means using the computer to process text and produce documents (Obj. 1)........	1.	**T**	**F**
2.	When doing word processing, errors may be corrected, but new words or sentences may not be added (Obj. 1)........	2.	**T**	**F**
3.	Groups of words are known as text (Obj. 1)........	3.	**T**	**F**
4.	A document is printed from text (Obj. 1)........	4.	**T**	**F**
5.	The diskette upon which text may be stored looks similar to a stereo record (Obj. 1)........	5.	**T**	**F**
6.	As you enter words into the computer, they are printed on paper by a printer (Obj. 1)........	6.	**T**	**F**
7.	All standard Apple II computers display 40 characters per line (Obj. 2)...	7.	**T**	**F**
8.	The Apple computer system consists of two parts: a keyboard and a printer (Obj. 2)........	8.	**T**	**F**
9.	Diskettes are durable and require no special handling (Obj. 3)........	9.	**T**	**F**
10.	If a diskette is not quite all the way into the disk drive, you should close the door to push it in (Obj. 3)........	10.	**T**	**F**
11.	*Apple Writer* is a computer program (Obj. 4)........	11.	**T**	**F**
12.	*Apple Writer* is a group of instructions that makes the computer behave as a word processor (Obj. 4)........	12.	**T**	**F**
13.	The *Apple Writer* diskette is inserted in the disk drive before the computer is turned on (Obj. 5)........	13.	**T**	**F**
14.	When quitting *Apple Writer*, the computer should be turned off before the diskette is removed from the disk drive (Obj. 5)........	14.	**T**	**F**

COMPLETION

1. What is the definition of word processing? (Obj. 1) ______________________

____

____

2. Describe each of the parts of the Apple computer system. (Obj. 2)
   Keyboard ______________________________
   Monitor ______________________________
   Disk Drive ______________________________
   Printer ______________________________
3. List six procedures for caring for diskettes. (Obj. 3)
   a. ______________________________
   b. ______________________________
   c. ______________________________
   d. ______________________________
   e. ______________________________
   f. ______________________________
4. What is *Apple Writer*? (Obj. 4) ______________________________
   ____
   ____
5. List the three steps that are necessary to power up the Apple computer. (Obj. 5)
   a. ______________________________
   b. ______________________________
   c. ______________________________
6. If your computer does not have an 80-column card or a shift key adapter installed, how do you answer *Apple Writer's* question *Do you have lower-case display (Y/N)?* (Obj. 5) ______________________________
7. List the keys that are struck to quit *Apple Writer*. (Obj. 5) ______________________________
   ____
8. How do you power down the Apple computer? (Obj. 5) ______________________________
   ____
   ____

COMPUTER EXERCISE

To complete this Computer Exercise, you will need an *Apple Writer* diskette and a student diskette. If these diskettes have not been given to you, ask your instructor for them. Then follow the steps below as you actually use the computer:

1. Turn on the monitor.
2. Insert the *Apple Writer* diskette into the disk drive. If there is more than one drive attached to the computer, remember to use Drive 1. If necessary, review the instructions in Step 2 on pages 4-5.
3. Turn on the power switch at the left rear of the computer. As soon as you turn on this switch, the disk drive will run for several seconds.
4. If the question *Do you have lowercase display (Y/N)?* appears on the screen, answer it by striking the Y or N key, then pressing RETURN.
5. When the message *Press RETURN to begin:* appears on the screen, press the RETURN key. The disk drive will run for several seconds. Then the Editor Menu will appear on the screen.
6. If your computer has one disk drive, remove the *Apple Writer* diskette from the disk drive and place the student diskette in the drive. If your computer has two disk drives, place the student diskette in Drive 2 rather than changing diskettes.
7. If your instructor has supplied you with a ready-to-use student diskette, skip this step. Otherwise, prepare the student diskette as follows:
   a. If it has not already been done, remove the *Apple Writer* diskette from its disk drive.
   b. Hold down the CTRL key while striking the O key. Be sure to strike the letter O and not the number zero. A display known as the DOS Commands menu will appear on the CRT.
   c. Select Option 6, which is the number of the *Initialize Diskette* option. You will then be required to enter a slot and drive number. If your new diskette is in Drive 1, key S6,D1. If your new diskette is in Drive 2, key S6,D2. Then press RETURN. (WARNING: Once you press RETURN, it is too late to change what you have done. If the diskette in the drive contains any information, it will be erased.) Once you press RETURN, the disk drive will run for a few seconds. Then the DOS Commands menu will

be redisplayed. Press RETURN to get back to the Editor Menu.

8. Quit *Apple Writer* by holding down the CTRL key while you strike the Q key. Then strike the 0 key (be sure to strike the number zero and not the letter O). The following question will appear on the screen: *Erases Memory. Quit(Y/N)?* Strike the Y key, then press RETURN.

9. When the lights on the disk drives go out, remove the diskettes and place each in its protective envelope.

You have now learned how to load *Apple Writer* and how to quit *Apple Writer*. In Lesson 2 you will create a document.

2. The Text Editor

OBJECTIVES:

1. Describe the Editor Menu.
2. Explain how to erase the memory of the computer.
3. Describe the functions of the Data Line.
4. State the purpose of the cursor.
5. List the methods of entering capital letters.
6. Describe what is meant by word wrap.
7. List the steps that are used in correcting errors with the backspace key.
8. Enter text using *Apple Writer.*

Many word processors, including *Apple Writer*, use **menus**. A menu is a list of functions the word processor can do. You choose the desired function by striking a certain key or keys. Once a menu option has been chosen, a status line or data line is often displayed at the top of the screen. The **data line** shows constantly updated information about your text. For example, it displays the length of your text. In this lesson, you will learn about *Apple Writer*'s Editor Menu and its Data Line. After learning the necessary steps, you will actually enter text into the computer.

THE EDITOR MENU

When the computer is powered up, the Editor Menu is displayed. The Editor Menu lists some of the more commonly used *Apple Writer* functions. Look at the illustration of the Editor Menu in Figure 2.1. In front of each function is a letter that is used to select that function. Note that the letters are enclosed in brackets. For example, *Load a file* is preceded by [*L*]. The brackets mean you must hold down the CTRL (control) key while striking the letter. It makes no difference whether the letter you strike while holding down CTRL is an uppercase or lowercase letter. These letters that are struck while holding down the CTRL key are known as **control characters**. Therefore, the options on the Editor Menu are called *Frequently Used Control Characters* rather than *Frequently Used Functions.* The various options on the Editor Menu will be discussed fully the first time you need to use each of them.

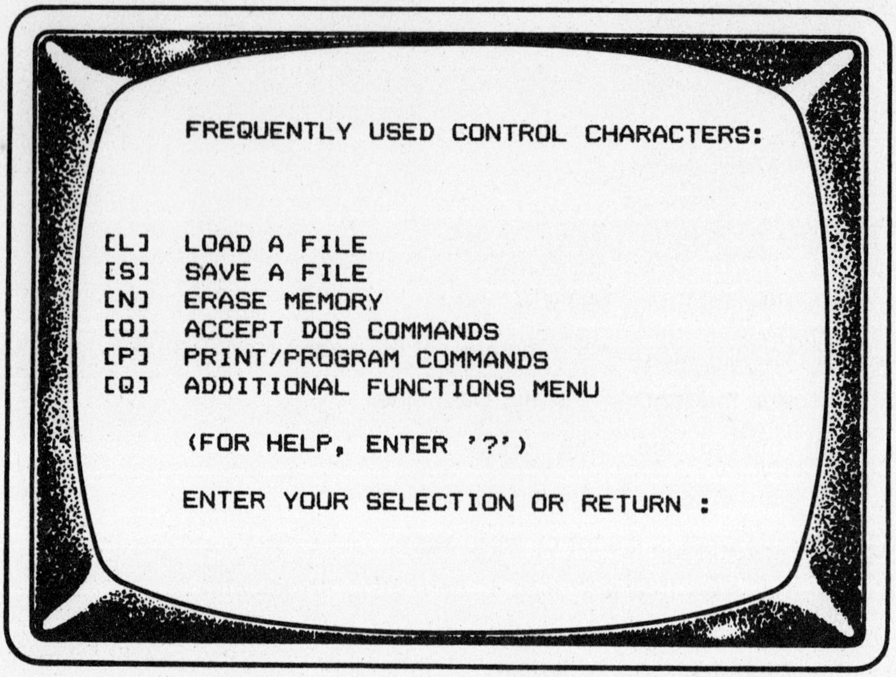

Figure 2.1 The Editor Menu

CREATING A DOCUMENT

Once the Editor Menu is displayed on the screen, you are ready to begin creating a document. The first step is to erase the memory of the computer.

Erasing Memory

Before entering text, you should erase the memory of the computer. This removes any old text that might accidentally become part of the new text. Look back at the Editor Menu in Figure 2.1. Note that the third option on the list is [*N*] *Erase memory.* By holding down the CTRL key and striking the N key, you are telling *Apple Writer* to erase the memory of the computer. Before actually erasing memory, *Apple Writer* will ask if that is what you really want. It will display the line [*N*]*ew (Erase Memory) Yes/No?* Key Yes and press RETURN.

The Data Line

When you enter [*N*] to erase the computer's memory, the screen is also cleared. A Data Line like the one in Figure 2.2 is then displayed at the top of the screen. The Data Line shows information about your text. Refer to Figure 2.2 as you read the following explanations of the items on the Data Line. On an Apple with an 80-column card, all the items appear on one line.

```
<E  Z MEM:19197 LEN:     0 POS:     0
TAB:     0 FILE:
```

Figure 2.2 The Data Line

MEM:. As text is entered into the computer, it is stored in the computer's memory. The number following *MEM:* on the Data Line tells how many more characters can be entered in the computer's memory before it is filled up. The *MEM:* figure at the time you begin entering text may vary depending on the amount of memory installed in your computer. As you enter text, the *MEM:* figure decreases.

LEN:. The number following *LEN:* shows the length of the text you have entered. If the Data Line reads *LEN: 398*, for example, you have entered 398 characters.

POS:. The number following *POS:* shows the current position of the cursor in the text you have entered. The **cursor** is a flashing rectangle that moves as you enter text, always showing the position at which the next character entered will be displayed. In this lesson, *POS:* will always show the same number as *LEN:* because the cursor will always be at the end of the text. In later lessons, when you have learned how to move the cursor so that words may be added, changed, or deleted, the two numbers may not be the same.

TAB:. The number following *TAB:* tells the number of characters you have entered since the last time you pressed RETURN.

The other items on the Data Line will be explained later as they are needed.

Entering Text

Whenever the Data Line and the cursor are on the screen, text may be entered. Before entering text, however, you should know about making capital letters, using word wrap, and correcting keying errors.

MAKING CAPITAL LETTERS. If you are using an Apple II, your computer may be standard, it may have a shift key adapter, or it may have an 80-column card. The capitalization of letters is different depending on which of these ways your computer is set up. (Note: Regardless of the method of making capital letters, you still use the SHIFT key for keying symbols and punctuation.) The following paragraphs explain the different methods for making capital letters.

Standard Apple II. Look at the Data Line in Figure 2.3. The *E* in the second position indicates that the ESC (escape) key must be used to capitalize letters. This is done by first striking the ESC key, then the letter to be capitalized (it is not necessary to hold the ESC key down while striking the letter). When you strike the ESC key, a ∧ (caret) symbol appears inside the cursor. This caret indicates that the next letter struck will appear as a capital letter when the document is printed. Remember that the standard Apple can display only uppercase letters on the screen. Therefore, letters that will be uppercase when the document is printed are shown on the screen as inverse (dark on light) characters. Letters that will appear on the document in lowercase are displayed on the screen as normal (light on dark) characters.

E shows that ESC key is used to make capital letters.

```
<E  Z MEM:19197 LEN:       0 POS:      0
TAB:      0 FILE:
```

Figure 2.3 Data Line of Standard Apple II

Apple II with Shift Key Adapter. If your Apple has a shift key adapter installed, you can make capital letters by using the SHIFT key. This is indicated on the Data Line by an *S* in the second position, as shown in Figure 2.4. You must hold down the SHIFT key while striking the letter to be capitalized. (Note: It is possible to turn the shift key adapter on and off. If you have a shift key adapter installed and the Data Line still shows *E* instead of *S*, follow these steps to turn on the adapter: First, enter [*Q*] to display the Additional Functions Menu. Then select Option 7, *Toggle Shift Key Option (ESC/SHIFT)*). As with the standard Apple II, all letters appear on the screen as uppercase. Those that will be uppercase on the document are shown in inverse on the screen. Those that will be lowercase on the document are shown on the screen as normal characters.

S shows that SHIFT key is used to make capital letters.

```
<S  Z MEM:19197 LEN:       0 POS:      0
TAB:      0 FILE:
```

Figure 2.4 Data Line with Shift Key Adapter or 80-Column Card Installed

Apple II with 80-Column Card. If your Apple has an 80-column card installed, capital letters are made by using the SHIFT key. This is indicated by an *S* in the second position on the Data Line (Figure 2.4). You must hold down the SHIFT key while striking the letter to be capitalized. The Apple II with an 80-column card displays both uppercase and lowercase letters on the screen.

WORD WRAP. If you have used an electric typewriter, you know that the RETURN key is pressed at the end of each line. This is not necessary when entering text with *Apple Writer*. When one line on the screen fills up, the text automatically wraps around to the next line. This means that when a word is too long to fit on a line, the entire word is moved automatically by the computer to the next line. Normally you should press RETURN only at points where your text *must* go to the next line. For example, you would press RETURN at the end of each line of the address of a letter, or at the end of each paragraph of a report. Word wrap increases your speed in entering text because you don't have to be concerned about margins.

When the letter *Z* appears before *MEM:* on the Data Line (Figure 2.4), it indicates that word wrap is turned on and working. However, if you want to turn word wrap off (when typing a table, for example), enter [*Z*]. To turn it back on, enter [*Z*] again.

CORRECTING ERRORS WITH THE BACKSPACE KEY. The simplest way of correcting errors is to use the backspace key. The backspace key is labeled on the keyboard with an arrow pointing left (←). Each time the backspace key is struck, the character to the left of the cursor is erased as the cursor passes over it. When you make an error, therefore, just backspace until the error disappears. Then reenter the correct text. Other methods of correcting errors will be explained in later lessons.

LESSON 2 EXERCISE

Name ______________________ Date ____________

TRUE/FALSE

Each of the following statements is either true or false. Indicate your choice in the Answers column by circling T for a true statement or F for a false statement.

	Answers
1. The Editor Menu is a list of some of *Apple Writer*'s more commonly used functions (Obj. 1)	1. **T F**
2. Control characters are entered by keying a bracket, the character, and another bracket (Obj. 1)	2. **T F**
3. The memory of the computer is erased by striking the CLEAR key (Obj. 2)	3. **T F**
4. The numbers on the Data Line include information about the length of the text (Obj. 3)	4. **T F**
5. The cursor enters characters into the computer's memory (Obj. 4)	5. **T F**
6. All capital letters are entered by using the SHIFT key (Obj. 5)	6. **T F**
7. Word wrap makes it unnecessary to press RETURN at the end of each line of a paragraph (Obj. 6)	7. **T F**
8. When using *Apple Writer*, the backspace key causes the cursor to move back without erasing the letters it passes over (Obj. 7)	8. **T F**

COMPLETION

1. Explain how to enter a control character. (Obj. 1) ______________________

____

2. Given below are the control characters that appear on the Editor Menu. Write the name of the function performed when each of the characters is entered. (Obj. 1)
   a. [L] ______________________
   b. [S] ______________________
   c. [N] ______________________
   d. [O] ______________________
   e. [P] ______________________
   f. [Q] ______________________

3. Using the following Data Line as an example, give the meaning of each of the indicated items. (Obj. 3)

```
<E Z MEM:19000 LEN:   197 POS:    197 TAB:     0 FILE:
```

   a. E in the second position ______________________
      S in the second position ______________________
   b. Z ______________________
   c. Mem: 19000 ______________________

d. Len: 197 ______

e. Pos: 197 ______

f. Tab: ______

4. What is the purpose of the cursor? (Obj. 4) ______

______

5. For each of the following types of computers, explain how to enter capital letters. (Obj. 5)
   a. Standard Apple II ______
   b. Apple II with shift key adapter ______
   c. Apple II with 80-column card ______

6. What is word wrap? (Obj. 6) ______

______

7. Explain how to correct keying errors using the backspace key. (Obj. 7) ______

______

______

COMPUTER EXERCISE

In this Computer Exercise, you will use *Apple Writer* to enter text into the computer. Follow the steps below as you use the computer:

1. Turn on the monitor.
2. Insert the *Apple Writer* diskette into the disk drive.
3. Turn on the computer's power switch.
4. If the question *Do you have lowercase display (Y/N)?* appears, answer it by striking the Y or N key as appropriate for your computer and pressing RETURN.
5. When the message, *Press RETURN to begin:* appears on the screen, press RETURN. The Editor Menu will appear on the screen.
6. If your computer has one disk drive, remove the *Apple Writer* diskette from the disk drive and insert the student diskette. If your computer has two disk drives, insert the student diskette in Drive 2 rather than changing diskettes.
7. Enter [*N*] to erase the computer's memory.
8. Enter the following text by keying it on the keyboard. If you make an error, backspace to the point of the error and rekey correctly. Do not press RETURN except at the end of each paragraph. Between paragraphs, press RETURN an extra time to get double spacing.

```
This is the first paragraph of text I have
keyed into the computer using a word
processor.  If I make a mistake, I will use
the backspace key to return to the error.
Then I will rekey the characters correctly.
In the next lesson I will learn how to enter
paragraphs with indentions.

I am learning how to use a word processor as
a powerful tool to help me in my work.  Use
of the computer will make my work much
easier since many of the routine tasks will
be done for me.
```

9. Quit *Apple Writer* by entering [*Q*]. Then strike the 0 key. Answer the question *Erases Memory. Quit (Y/N)?* with a Y and press RETURN.
10. Remove the student diskette from the disk drive and place it in its protective envelope. If the *Apple Writer* diskette is still in Drive 1, remove it also.
11. Power down the computer by turning off the power switches on the monitor and computer.

3. Entering Text

OBJECTIVES:

1. Describe the procedure for entering special symbols.
2. Describe the procedure for using alpha lock.
3. Describe the procedure for setting, clearing, and using tab stops.
4. Enter text with indented paragraphs, uppercase words, and special symbols.

In Lesson 2 you learned to enter simple text. Most word processing, however, requires more complex text. In this lesson, you will learn some ways to enter such text. You will enter special symbols, use the alphabetic shift lock, and use tab stops.

ENTERING SPECIAL SYMBOLS

Special symbols are nonalphabetic characters on the keyboard such as $, &, and %. Each one is entered by holding down the SHIFT key while striking the appropriate character key. You follow this procedure even if your computer requires the use of the ESC key to enter uppercase letters.

ALPHA LOCK

At times you may want to capitalize several letters in a row. For example, the main heading of a report might be in all uppercase letters. Use of alpha lock (known also as alphabetic shift lock) allows you to enter such a series of uppercase letters without striking ESC or the SHIFT key for each letter. To use alpha lock on the Apple IIe, depress the key labeled CAPS LOCK. On the Apple II, enter [*K*]. The letter *U* (for uppercase) will appear on the Data Line in place of the *E* or *S*, as in Figure 3.1. Now all of the letters you enter will be in uppercase. To return to normal uppercase and lowercase operation on the Apple IIe, depress the CAPS LOCK key again. On the Apple II, enter [*K*] again to turn off alpha lock. As an example for the Apple II, to enter a title in all capitals you might key [*K*]*HOW TO USE YOUR WORD PROCESSOR*[*K*]. Use of alpha lock does not shift the numeric keys to their symbols. To enter the special characters on the numeric keys you must still use the SHIFT key.

U means that alpha lock (uppercase) is in use.

```
<U  Z MEM:19197 LEN:      0 POS:      0
TAB:     0 FILE:
```

Figure 3.1 Data Line with Alpha Lock in Use

USING TAB STOPS

Apple Writer provides tab stops similar to those on a typewriter. When you load *Apple Writer*, it automatically sets nine tab stops that are eight columns apart. These are known as default tab stops. Entering [*I*] (for indent) moves the cursor to the next tab stop. You may clear and set new tabs at any desired column positions if the default stops are not suitable. To clear all tab stops, enter [*T*] (for tab). When you do this, the screen will display [*T*]*ab(Set/Clear/Purge):* Enter *P*, which stands for purge, and all tab stops will be cleared. The prompt line will also be erased. You may then continue with the next desired step, which probably will be to set one or more new tab stops.

To set a tab stop, you must first move the cursor to the desired column number. As you move the cursor by striking the space bar, watch the number after *TAB:* on the Data Line. When this number corresponds to the column at which you want to set a tab, enter [*T*]. In response to the [*T*]*ab(Set/Clear/Purge):* prompt, enter an *S* for set. If you want to set additional tabs, move the cursor to the next column at which you want a tab stop and repeat the process. Note that tab stop columns are counted from the last time you pressed RETURN, not from the left edge of the screen. Therefore, you can set a tab at a column number larger than the width of the screen.

To clear a single tab stop, tab (using [*I*]) until the cursor is at the column to be cleared, then enter [*T*]. In response to the [*T*]*ab(Set/Clear/Purge):* prompt, enter *C* for clear. Only this tab stop will be cleared.

LESSON 3 EXERCISE Name ______________________ Date __________

TRUE/FALSE

Each of the following statements is either true or false. Indicate your choice in the Answers column by circling T for a true statement or F for a false statement.

		Answers		
1.	Special symbols are nonalphabetic characters (Obj. 1)	1.	**T**	**F**
2.	Computers that require the use of ESC to make capital letters also require ESC to make special symbols (Obj. 1)	2.	**T**	**F**
3.	Alpha lock shifts special symbols to numeric characters (Obj. 2)	3.	**T**	**F**
4.	Alpha lock is turned on by striking the ESC key twice (Obj. 2)	4.	**T**	**F**
5.	When alpha lock is turned on, an *S* appears on the Data Line (Obj. 2) ...	5.	**T**	**F**
6.	After you enter a word in capital letters, you use [*K*] to turn off the alpha lock feature of *Apple Writer* (Obj. 2)	6.	**T**	**F**
7.	Alpha lock shifts number keys to their special symbols (Obj. 2)	7.	**T**	**F**
8.	You may not set tabs at column positions greater than 40 since the screen has only 40 columns (Obj. 3)	8.	**T**	**F**
9.	To set or clear a tab stop, you enter [*T*], which stands for tab (Obj. 3) ...	9.	**T**	**F**
10.	To clear all tab stops, you must move the cursor to each one and strike the CLEAR key (Obj. 3)	10.	**T**	**F**
11.	The TAB key may be used to indent paragraphs on the Apple II (Obj. 3)	11.	**T**	**F**
12.	After telling *Apple Writer* you want to clear a tab stop, you move the cursor to the column you want to clear (Obj. 3)	12.	**T**	**F**

COMPLETION

For each of the following functions, write the key or combination of keys that should be used. Remember to write brackets around any keys that are control characters. Answer each question for the computer you are using: either the Apple II or Apple IIe.

Function	Keys
1. Entering a symbol such as *$* (Obj. 1)	1. ______________________
2. Entering *COMPUTER* in all capital letters (Obj. 2)	2. ______________________
3. Entering *MODEL 3987BA* (Obj. 2)	3. ______________________
4. Clearing all the tab stops (Obj. 3)	4. ______________________
5. Setting a tab stop at Column 5 (Obj. 3)	5. ______________________
6. Clearing a tab stop at Column 24 (Obj. 3)	6. ______________________

COMPUTER EXERCISE

In this Computer Exercise, you will enter a short report. Enter its heading in all capital letters. Special symbols are included in the report. Follow the steps below as you use the computer:

1. Turn on the monitor.
2. Insert the *Apple Writer* diskette into the disk drive.
3. Turn on the computer's power switch.
4. If the question *Do you have lowercase display (Y/N)?* appears, answer it by entering *Y* or *N* as appropriate for your computer.
5. When the message *Press RETURN to begin:* appears on the screen, press RETURN. The Editor Menu will appear on the screen.
6. If your computer has one disk drive, remove the *Apple Writer* diskette from the disk drive and insert the student diskette. If your computer has two disk drives, insert the student diskette into Drive 2 instead of changing diskettes.
7. Enter [*N*] to erase the computer's memory.
8. Clear all of *Apple Writer*'s tab stops. Begin by entering [*T*]. When prompted, enter *P* (which stands for purge).
9. Set a new tab stop at Column 5. To do this, strike the space bar until a *5* is displayed after *TAB:* on the Data Line display. Then enter [*T*] and an *S*.
10. Enter the following text. Remember to use the alpha lock to enter words in all caps. Use [*I*] to indent the paragraphs; don't strike the space bar five times to indent them. If you make an error, backspace to the point of the error and rekey correctly. Do not press RETURN except at the end of each paragraph. Between paragraphs, press RETURN an extra time to get double spacing.

MY APPLE COMPUTER

The Apple computer can be used to do word processing. The computer follows a program (set of instructions) that tells it what to do. Some writers say using the computer to do word processing can save them from 75% to 80% of their time.

To get the computer started, a disk is inserted into Drive #1 and the power switch is turned on. Since the 5¼" disk is so important, it should be PROTECTED from harm at all times. Do not bend it, touch its exposed surfaces, or expose it to low or high temperatures. Temperatures > 125 degrees or < 50 degrees must be avoided. If you treat your disk carefully, it will serve you for a long time.

[S]ave: Name

11. Ask your instructor to examine your work. Do not erase your work or quit *Apple Writer* until told to do so by your instructor.

[N] Clear Memory Y N

12. When told to do so by your instructor, quit *Apple Writer* by entering [*Q*]. Then strike the 0 (zero) key. Answer the question *Erases Memory. Quit(Y/N)?* with Y and press RETURN.

Type Y

13. Remove the student diskette from the disk drive and place it in its protective envelope. If the student diskette was in Drive 2, also remove the *Apple Writer* diskette from Drive 1 and place it in its envelope.
14. Power down the computer.

4. Saving Text

OBJECTIVES:

1. Describe the method by which text is recorded on the diskette.
2. Define a file and tell its purpose.
4. Describe the procedure for saving a file.
4. Describe the procedure for displaying a diskette catalog.
5. State the meaning of each of the items in a diskette catalog.

Once you have entered text, you may save it on diskette. This capability is one of the outstanding features of a word processing system. By recalling text from the disk, you can make changes without reentering the entire document.

In this lesson, you will learn basic information about saving or recording text. Then you will learn the steps for saving text with *Apple Writer*.

HOW TEXT IS RECORDED ON THE DISKETTE

As you learned earlier, a diskette is coated with magnetic material similar to that on a cassette tape. Magnetic spots are placed on the diskette during the recording process. Each character (letter, number, or symbol) has its own combination of magnetic spots recorded on the diskette.

On a diskette, the magnetic spots are recorded in circles within circles (concentric circles). Note in Figure 4.1 that these circles cover the outer area of the diskette. Each of the circles is known as a track. Each track is divided into short lengths called sectors; that is, one track may be divided into 16 recording areas, each able to save 256 characters. When saving text, the computer uses as many of these sectors as are required to hold all the information. In other words, brief text requires less space than longer text.

DEFINITION OF A FILE

The text for a document is known as a **file** when it is stored on a diskette. The computer keeps track of the location of empty space on the diskette and records text there. For the computer to do this, you must make up a different name for each file when you save it. The computer then enters the file name into the diskette catalog or directory. The catalog is quite similar to the table of contents of a book. It contains information about the length and type of each file.

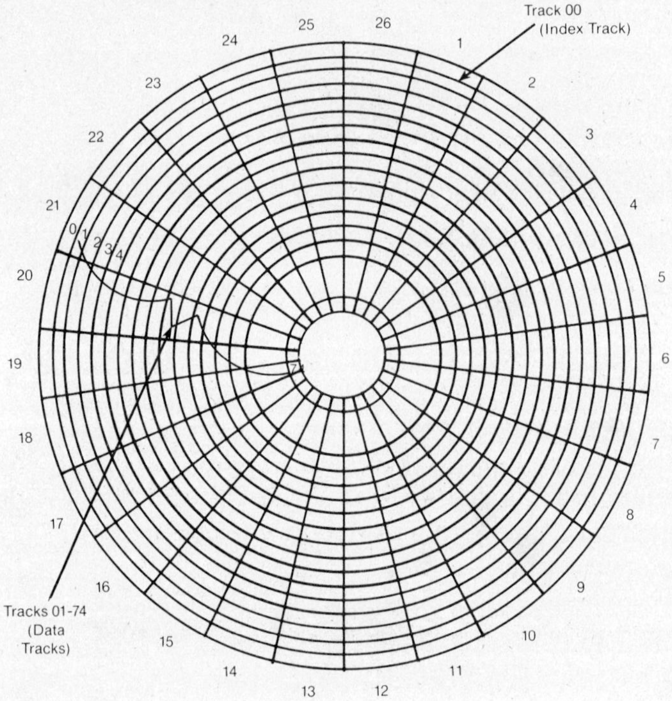

Figure 4.1 Illustration of Tracks and Sectors on a Diskette

USING FILES

As text is entered on the keyboard, it is stored in the computer's memory. When you have finished entering text (or before you come to the end of your text, if you wish) the text can be **saved**. This means it is copied from the computer's memory onto the diskette. Saved text is stored for future use and is known as a file. Even when you erase the text from the computer's memory or turn off the computer, the file remains on the diskette. When you want to work with it again, you ask the computer to load (copy) the file from the diskette into the computer's memory.

STEPS IN SAVING A FILE

Once you have entered text with *Apple Writer*, it can be saved on diskette. The next sections describe the steps in saving a file.

Assigning a File Name

The first step in saving a file with *Apple Writer* is to assign it a file name. The file name is a word or title by which the text will be known on the diskette. The file name may be anything you want it to be as long as it fits the following rules:

1. The file name must begin with a letter. (*Apple Writer* converts all letters in file names to uppercase. Therefore, it makes no difference whether you enter the name in uppercase or lowercase.)
2. The file name cannot contain more than 30 characters.
3. The file name cannot contain a comma.

Here are some good file names:

LETTER 1 *SMITH/R 4/4/84* *CHAPTER 3* *LESSON 12 ALICE VOGEL*

Here are some file names that may not be used, along with the reasons:

INVALID FILE NAMES	REASONS
4/4/84 LETTER	Does not begin with a letter
PROPOSAL TO THE HILLSBOROUGH SCHOOL BOARD	Has more than 30 characters
SMITH,R WILL	Contains a comma

If you use the name of a file that already exists on the diskette, the text in the original file will be replaced by the new text. Therefore, before deciding on a file name, it is a good idea to look at a list of all files already saved on diskette. The way to do this is explained later in this lesson in the section "Using the Diskette Catalog."

Assigning a Disk Drive Number

If your computer has only one disk drive, all files will be saved on the diskette that is in that drive. If you have two disk drives, however, files may be saved on the diskette in either drive. As you know, the drive into which you place the *Apple Writer* diskette is Drive 1. The second drive is known as Drive 2. In this course, you should always save files using the drive into which you have placed your student diskette.

Saving a File on the Diskette

After you select a file name and determine which disk drive your student diskette is in, you are ready to save a file. You may save the text that you are entering at any time you wish. The saving process does not erase the text from memory. Therefore, you can continue making changes after saving the text. You must remember, however, to save the text again after making the changes. The new version will then replace the old version on the diskette.

To save your text, enter the [*S*] (save) command. *Apple Writer* will display [*S*]*ave:* at the bottom of the screen. Enter the name you have decided to use for the file in which the text will be saved. If you want to use Drive 2, enter a comma and D2 after the file name. Here are some examples of file names you might enter after the [*S*]*ave:* prompt:

To save on Drive 1 *TERM PAPER ENGLISH 401*
To save on Drive 2 *TERM PAPER ENGLISH 401,D2*

Note that it is not necessary to enter D1 when using Drive 1, although you may do so if you wish. When you key the file name and press RETURN, the disk drive will operate briefly while the file is being saved. The red light on the front of the drive will show that it is running. When the computer finishes saving the file, its name will be displayed on the Data Line after the word *FILE:*.

USING THE DISKETTE CATALOG

A list of the files stored on diskette is known as a **diskette catalog**. In addition to the names of the files, the catalog contains other important information. You display the diskette catalog on the screen by entering [*O*] (be sure you strike the letter O and not the number zero). When you enter [*O*], the DOS Commands menu will appear on the screen as in Figure 4.2. DOS stands for Disk Operating System. It is the master program built into your Apple computer that directs and controls the operation of the computer and other programs such as *Apple Writer*. Among its functions are those shown on the DOS Commands menu.

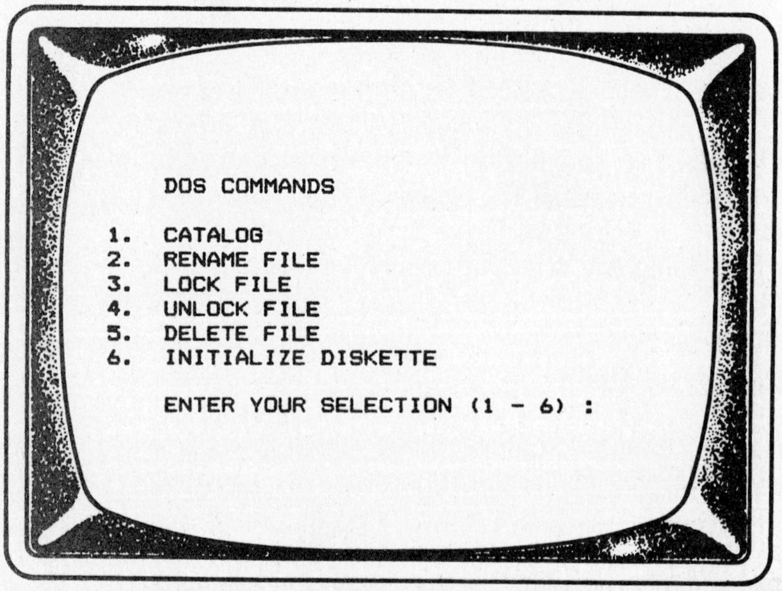

Figure 4.2 DOS Commands Menu

When the DOS Commands menu is displayed, select Option 1 and press RETURN. You may then be asked to enter a slot number and drive number. The slot number is the location inside the computer where the circuit card that controls the disk drive is plugged in. If the circuit cards inside your Apple are plugged into the standard positions, the slot number is 6. The drive number is either 1 or 2. (The drive number should be attached to the front of the disk drive. If you have only one drive, it is always Drive 1.) Enter the figures as *S6,D1* or *S6,D2*. (If you want to see the catalog of Drive 1, you may also simply press RETURN without entering the numbers.) The disk drive will run briefly, then the diskette catalog will be displayed. After viewing it, press RETURN again and the DOS Commands Menu will be redisplayed. If you press RETURN instead of making a choice from the menu, your text will be redisplayed on the screen.

Refer to the typical diskette catalog shown in Figure 4.3. The Disk Volume number of 254 is a number assigned to the diskette at the time it was created. If you desire to do so, you may specify a number when you initialize a diskette. Otherwise, *Apple Writer* will use 254. The T at the beginning of the line for each file entry means that the file is a text file. All text files created with *Apple Writer* will be type T. Files containing tab and margin settings will be type B (binary or machine language files). If a diskette contains computer programs written in the BASIC language, you will see file types of A (created by Applesoft BASIC) or I (created by Apple's Integer BASIC).

```
DISK VOLUME 254

*T 006 BERTRAND WILL
 T 021 W77 4
 T 014 WALLACE LETTER 042484

                    (PRESS RETURN)
```

Figure 4.3 Typical Diskette Catalog

Refer again to Figure 4.3. The number following the T tells you the size of the file. The size is given in sectors. Remember that each sector holds 256 characters. Therefore, multiply the given file size by 256 to find the approximate number of characters in the entire file. For example, the file called *BERTRAND WILL* has a file size of 6 sectors. Multiplying the 6 by 256 gives 1536, the approximate number of characters in the file. Since the last sector may not be completely filled, the calculated number of characters may be slightly higher than the actual number of characters in the file. Following the file size on the diskette catalog is the name of the file assigned at the time it was saved.

The asterisk at the very beginning of the line for the file named *BERTRAND WILL* indicates that the file is locked. A locked file cannot be changed or deleted unless it is first unlocked. In Lesson 9 you will learn how to lock and unlock files.

LESSON 4 EXERCISE Name ______________________ Date __________

TRUE/FALSE

Each of the following statements is either true or false. Indicate your choice in the Answers column by circling T for a true statement or F for a false statement.

	Answers		
1. A diskette is coated with magnetic material (Obj. 1)	1.	T	F
2. Each character is stored on a diskette as a combination of magnetic spots (Obj. 1)	2.	T	F
3. Sectors on a diskette are divided into recording tracks (Obj. 1)	3.	T	F
4. When the text for a document is stored on diskette, it is known as a file (Obj. 2)	4.	T	F
5. All files on diskettes require the same amount of space (Obj. 2)	5.	T	F
6. When you command the computer to save a file, it gets a name for the file from its index (Obj. 2)	6.	T	F
7. Text saved in a file on a diskette may be read back into the computer's memory at a later time (Obj. 2)	7.	T	F
8. A file name may be whatever length you desire (Obj. 3)	8.	T	F
9. File names may not contain commas (Obj. 3)	9.	T	F
10. The command that is used to save a file onto diskette is [*F*] (for file) (Obj. 3)	10.	T	F
11. The computer keeps track of the location and amount of available space on the diskette (Obj. 3)	11.	T	F
12. The diskette catalog is a list of the files stored on a diskette (Obj. 4)	12.	T	F
13. The diskette catalog is displayed by selecting an option from the Additional Functions Menu (Obj. 4)	13.	T	F
14. *Apple Writer*'s diskette catalog shows the exact location of each file on the disk (Obj. 4)	14.	T	F

COMPLETION

Following is a typical entry from a diskette catalog. Using the entry as an example, write the meaning of each of the items on the lines below. (Obj. 5).

```
*T 172 MASTER CONTRACT 1985
```

1. * ______________________________
2. T ______________________________
3. 172 ______________________________
4. MASTER CONTRACT 1985 ______________________________

COMPUTER EXERCISE

In this Computer Exercise, you will enter a personal note. You will then save it in a file on diskette. Follow the steps below as you use the computer. (Note: This is the last lesson in which detailed instructions for powering up the computer will be given.)

1. Turn on the monitor.
2. Insert the *Apple Writer* diskette into the disk drive.
3. Turn on the computer's power switch.
4. If the question, *Do you have lowercase display (Y/N):* appears, answer it by entering *Y* or *N* as appropriate for your computer.
5. When the message *Press RETURN to begin:* appears on the screen, press RETURN. The Editor Menu menu will be displayed on the screen.
6. If your computer has one disk drive, remove the *Apple Writer* diskette from the disk drive and insert the student diskette. If your computer has two disk drives, insert the student diskette into Drive 2 instead of changing diskettes.
7. Enter [*N*] to erase the computer's memory.
8. Clear all of *Apple Writer*'s tab stops. Begin by entering [*T*] (for tab). When prompted, enter *P* (which stands for purge).
9. Set a new tab stop at Column 5. To do this, strike the space bar five times. Then enter [*T*] and an *S* (for set).
10. Enter the following text. Remember to use the alpha lock ([*K*]) to enter any words that are in all caps. Use [*T*] to indent the paragraphs. If you make an error, backspace to the point of the error and rekey correctly. Press RETURN only at the end of each paragraph. Between paragraphs press RETURN an extra time to get a blank line between the paragraphs.

```
Dear Pat

     It was great to receive a holiday note
from you.  We've really missed you since you
moved to WARM Florida.  I know you're
enjoying the sunny shores at Daytona.

     Up here in snow country, we have almost
become accustomed to our annual blizzard.  It
arrived with full fury last night.  We now
have almost three feet of snow on the ground.
```

11. Enter [*S*]. This tells *Apple Writer* that you want to save your text. The prompt [*S*]*ave:* will appear at the bottom of the screen. *Apple Writer* is now waiting for you to enter the name and disk drive number for storing your file. For the file name, use the lesson number followed by your name. For example, you might enter *LESSON 4 LEE SMITH.* If your student diskette is in Drive 2, remember to place a comma and the drive number at the end of your file name. For example, you might enter *LESSON 4 LEE SMITH,D2*. As soon as you have entered the file name (and drive number if necessary), press RETURN. The disk drive will run briefly while your text is being saved. When the light on the disk drive goes out, your text has been saved.

12. Look at a catalog of the diskette to see that your file has been saved. Enter [*O*], then a *1*. When asked for the slot and drive numbers, enter *S6,D1* or *S6,D2*, depending on which drive contains your student diskette. The diskette catalog will be displayed. Find your file in the listing. Press RETURN twice to get back to your text.

13. Quit *Apple Writer* by entering [*Q*]. Then strike the 0 (zero) key. Answer the question *Erases Memory, Quit (Y/N)?* with a *Y* and press RETURN.

14. Remove the student diskette from the disk drive and place it in its protective envelope. If the student diskette was in Drive 2, also remove the *Apple Writer* diskette from Drive 1 and place it in its envelope. Power down the computer. The text file you saved in this lesson will be used again in Lesson 5.

5. Loading and Printing Text

OBJECTIVES:

1. List the steps to use in loading a file.
2. Describe the procedure for making changes to a file loaded from diskette.
3. Describe how to print a file.
4. Practice loading, changing, and printing a file.

Text that has been saved on a diskette may be loaded into the computer's memory and printed whenever you wish. If necessary, additions or changes may be made in the text before the document is printed. The changed text may also be saved to the diskette before printing, if desired.

STEPS IN LOADING A FILE

Loading a file refers to the process of reading text from a diskette and placing it into the computer's memory. The following paragraphs describe the steps in loading a file.

Looking at the Diskette Catalog

If you remember the name of the file you want to load into memory, you may immediately load it. Frequently, however, you may not be sure of the file name. In that case, you need to display the diskette catalog to see the file name. As you learned in Lesson 4, the first step in looking at the diskette catalog is to enter [*O*]. This displays the DOS Commands menu. From this menu, select Option 1 (*Catalog*).

Erasing the Computer's Memory

On most occasions, you will want to erase the computer's memory before loading a document. If this is not done, the text you load will be combined with any text already in memory. Remember that the first step in erasing the computer's memory is to enter [*N*]. Then, enter a *Y* when asked whether you want to erase memory.

Loading a File from Memory

As soon as you have erased the computer's memory, you are ready to load the file from diskette into memory. This is done by entering [*L*], which stands for load. At the bottom of the screen, *Apple Writer* will display [*L*]*OAD:* This is your prompt to enter the file name and disk drive number. Simply key in the name that was used for storing the file on diskette. For example, for a file stored on a diskette in Drive 1 you might enter *MAX MCBRAYER CONTRACT*. For a file stored on a diskette in Drive 2, follow the file name with the drive number. For example, after [*L*]*OAD:* you might enter *MAX MCBRAYER CONTRACT,D2*. The disk drive will run briefly. Then you will see your text displayed on the CRT.

SAVING TEXT USING THE FILE NAME ON THE DATA LINE

Many times you will want to make changes in your text before printing it. If so, all the editing functions you have learned may be used on the text loaded from diskette. If the changes are temporary, you may make the changes and then print the document. If the changes are permanent, you will want to save the revised text before printing it.

If you want to save the revised text under the same file name from which it was loaded, *Apple Writer* provides a convenient shortcut. When you load a file from diskette, the name of the file is displayed on the Data Line. The word *FILE:* precedes the name. Look at the Data Line in Figure 5.1. The name of the file loaded from diskette is *LESSON 4 RODNEY BROWN*.

```
<E  Z MEM:18997 LEN:   200 POS:    49
TAB:      0 FILE:LESSON 4 RODNEY BROWN
```

Figure 5.1 Data Line of Standard Apple Showing File Name

If you want to replace the original file on diskette with the changed text, enter [*S*] as usual for saving a file. Instead of entering a file name, however, enter an equals sign (=). The equals sign tells *Apple Writer* to use the name from the Data Line to save the text. (Note: When originally entering lengthy text, it is a good idea to save your work every few minutes. Once you have saved the text the first time, the file name will be on the Data Line, and the equals sign may be used each time you save the text instead of reentering the file name.)

PRINTING A FILE

Text may be printed any time it is in memory. It makes no difference whether you have just entered the text or whether you loaded it from diskette. It is a good idea, however, to always save your text on diskette before printing it. That way, if the computer system does not function properly during printing, your work will not be lost.

Once the text to be printed is in memory, you should check to make sure your printer is ready by following these steps:

1. Be sure the printer is plugged in and turned on.
2. Make sure that there is paper in the printer and that the paper is lined up at the point where you want printing to begin.
3. If the printer has an on-line switch, make sure it is in the on-line position.

After you verify that the printer is ready, enter [*P*], which stands for print. At the bottom of the screen *Apple Writer* will display the prompt [*P*]*RINT/PROGRAM:* Enter the two letters *NP*, which stand for new print. This tells the computer that you want printing to begin on the new page you have positioned in the printer. After you have entered *NP*, press RETURN and the printer will begin to work. If it does not start, recheck the items listed earlier.

Note: Depending on how your printer is connected to the computer, text that is being printed may also appear on the screen. If this is the case, the printed lines will probably be shorter than desired. To remedy this situation, enter the following as the first line of your text: [*V*][*I*][*V*]*80N*. Remember that the brackets mean to hold down the CTRL (control) key while striking the letter. Press RETURN after entering the line.

If you need to stop the printer while it is printing, strike the ESC (escape) key. The printer will stop and the Editor Menu will be displayed. Pressing RETURN will then redisplay your text.

When printing is finished, you may take any action desired. For example, you can make more changes in the text, print another copy, erase memory and work on different text, or quit *Apple Writer*.

LESSON 5 EXERCISE Name ______________________ Date __________

TRUE/FALSE

Each of the following statements is either true or false. Indicate your choice in the Answers column by circling T for a true statement or F for a false statement.

		Answers	
1.	If you cannot remember the name you used when you saved a file, it is impossible to load the file (Obj. 1)	1. T	F
2.	When you are prompted to enter a slot and drive number, you may just press RETURN if you are using Drive 1 (Obj. 1)	2. T	F
3.	On most occasions, the computer's memory should be erased before loading a file from diskette (Obj. 1)	3. T	F
4.	You must display the diskette catalog before loading a file from diskette (Obj. 1)	4. T	F
5.	The command for loading a file is [*F*] (for file) (Obj. 1)	5. T	F
6.	Once a file is loaded from diskette, all of *Apple Writer*'s editing functions may be used to make changes in the text (Obj. 2)	6. T	F
7.	If a file name is shown on the Data Line, the equals sign may be used instead of the file name to resave the text under the name shown on the Data Line (Obj. 2)	7. T	F
8.	A document may be printed at any time its text is in the computer's memory (Obj. 3)	8. T	F
9.	When [*P*] is entered, printing starts immediately (Obj. 3)	9. T	F
10.	*NP* (new print) is used to tell *Apple Writer* to stop printing after each page so that the paper may be changed (Obj. 3)	10. T	F

COMPLETION

For each of the following functions, write in the Keys column the key or combination of keys that should be used, including file names. Remember to write brackets around any control characters. Assume that the file name is CSC CONTRACT, and that it is saved on Drive 1.

Function	Keys
1. Displaying the diskette catalog (Obj. 1)	1. ______________
2. Erasing the computer's memory (Obj. 1)	2. ______________
3. Loading a file (Obj. 1)	3. ______________
4. Saving a changed file using the name on the Data Line (Obj.2)	4. ______________
5. Printing a file that is in memory (Obj. 3)	5. ______________
6. Stopping printing (Obj. 3)	6. ______________

COMPUTER EXERCISE

In this Computer Exercise, you will load the file that you created in Lesson 4. You will then add a paragraph, save the changed text, and print the document. Follow the steps below as you use the computer:

1. Power up the computer. If necessary, review the steps given in the Computer Exercise in Lesson 4. After loading *Apple Writer*, be sure you place the student diskette into the disk drive.
2. Display the student diskette catalog and look at the name under which you stored your text from Lesson 4. To do this, first enter [*O*]. Then strike the 1 key. When prompted, press RETURN if your student diskette is in Drive 1. If it is in Drive 2, enter the slot and drive number (S6,D2). Find the name of your file on the screen and remember it. Then press RETURN twice to redisplay the Data Line.
3. Load your file from Lesson 4. Begin by entering [*L*]. When prompted at the bottom of the screen, enter the file name you found on the diskette catalog. If your student diskette is in Drive 2, enter *,D2* (comma D2) after the file name and press RETURN. The disk drive will run briefly; then your text will be displayed on the screen.
4. Press RETURN, then clear all of *Apple Writer*'s tab stops by entering [*T*], then *P* (for purge). Set a new tab stop at Column 5 for the paragraph indention. To do this, strike the space bar five times. The enter [*T*] and an *S* (for set).
5. Press RETURN to get a blank line after the last paragraph on the screen. Then add the following paragraph to the end of the note. Enter [*I*] to indent the paragraph. Remember to press RETURN only at the end of the paragraph, not at the end of each line.

```
    Perhaps you can come up for a visit in
the summer.  If you wait until it is warm, we
can go skiing on Lake George.  Won't that be
great fun!  Give me a call and let me know
when you can come.  The boat and skiis are
waiting.
```

6. Save the new version of the note on the diskette under the same name used in Lesson 4. This means that all three paragraphs of your personal note will replace the original two paragraphs on the diskette. First, enter [*S*]

to tell *Apple Writer* you want to save the text. Since the file name is displayed on the Data Line, you may enter an equals sign (=) instead of the file name when prompted.

7. Make sure the printer is plugged in, turned on, on-line (if there is an on-line switch), and has paper lined up where you want the printing to begin.
8. Enter [*P*] for print. When the [*P*]*RINT/PROGRAM:* prompt is displayed, enter *NP* (for new print) and press RETURN. Printing should begin. If it does not, recheck the printer. If necessary, ask your instructor.
9. When the printing is finished, quit *Apple Writer* and power down the computer.

6. Basic Editing

OBJECTIVES:

1. Explain how to position the cursor using the cursor movement keys.
2. Explain how to change the direction arrow.
3. Describe the procedure for inserting text.
4. Describe the procedure for deleting text.

The heart of any word processing system is the ability to **edit**, or change, text. Editing includes correcting errors, inserting text, and deleting text. You have already learned to edit text as you enter it by using the backspace key to strike over errors. Once you have entered text, it should also be proofread and edited before the final version is saved on diskette. Text that has been saved on diskette can be loaded and edited, and then the new version can be saved. Editing saves time in the preparation of a document since you can change the data stored in the memory of the computer as many times as necessary before you print the document. Additional changes can be made to the text file after the document is printed if desired.

CURSOR CONTROL

After you enter text, you should proofread it on the screen before it is printed or saved on diskette. Errors that you did not correct while you were entering the text should be corrected at this time. *Apple Writer* enables you to move the cursor to positions in the text where corrections are to be made without erasing text that is already correct. To do this, you change the cursor from normal text-entry mode to move mode by striking the ESC key twice. (Note: If the shift key adapter or the 80-column card has been installed in your computer, strike the ESC key only once.) The @ symbol will appear inside the cursor. This indicates that the cursor is in move mode instead of text-entry mode. You can now move the cursor to any place on the screen by using the following keys:

Key	Cursor Movement
I	Up one line
J	Left one character
K	Right one character
M	Down one line
E	Up 12 lines
S	Left 24 characters
D	Right 24 characters
X	Down 12 lines

The cursor can be moved rapidly from one location to another by striking any one of the keys above and the REPT (repeat) key at the same time. On an Apple IIe, the cursor is moved rapidly by simply holding down any one of the keys above.

Notice that the keys E, S, D, and X on the left side of the keyboard are in the same arrangement as the keys I, J, K, and M on the right side. Labeling these keys will help you to remember their functions. In addition, to help remember the keys, note that their arrangement on the keyboard corresponds to their functions (up, down, left, and right).

Figure 6.1 Cursor Movement Keys

SCROLLING

The *Apple Writer* screen displays 22 lines of text at any time. However, the cursor moves down only to the thirteenth line and remains on the thirteenth line as you enter text. Because this position is the approximate middle of the screen, it helps to reduce eye fatigue. After the thirteenth line has been entered, the text **scrolls** upward. In other words, it moves to the top of the screen and disappears. You have not lost the text, however, because it is still stored in memory. If you wish to see text that is not on the screen, use the cursor movement keys. As you move the cursor up, the text scrolls down.

You can quickly move the cursor to either the beginning or the end of the text. To move the cursor to the beginning of the text, enter [*B*] (for beginning). The cursor will be immediately positioned at the beginning of the text. Notice that this command sets the first character on the Data Line (called a direction arrow) to >. To quickly move the cursor to the end of the text, enter [*E*] (for end). This command sets the direction arrow to <. The direction arrow can be changed at any time to either direction by entering [*D*] (for direction). The direction arrow is used with special editing functions that will be explained in the next lesson.

INSERTING TEXT

You can make changes to text by inserting or deleting characters, words, or paragraphs. To insert text, use the ESC key to change the cursor to move mode. Then position the cursor where the text is to be inserted by using the cursor movement keys. Strike the space bar to return the cursor to text-entry mode. You are now ready to insert text by entering the information on the keyboard. As you enter the new text, the text to the right of the cursor will be moved across the line and down the screen to make room for the additional text.

DELETING TEXT

There are three ways to delete text on the screen: by character, by word, and by paragraph. In Lesson 2 you learned how to delete characters. This method can also be used in combination with the cursor movement keys. To delete a character or a series of characters, first use the ESC key to change the cursor to move mode. Then position the cursor to the right of the character to be deleted, using the cursor movement keys. Strike the backspace key once for each character or space to be deleted, as you learned in Lesson 2. If several characters in a row are to be deleted, hold the backspace key and the REPT key down at the same time. (On the Apple IIe simply hold down the backspace key.) Be careful using this method as the cursor moves quickly and may delete more than is desired. If this should happen, use the procedures described above for inserting text. The other two methods of deleting text will be discussed in the next lesson.

LESSON 6 EXERCISE Name ______________________ Date __________

TRUE/FALSE

Each of the following statements is either true or false. Indicate your choice in the Answers column by circling T for a true statement or F for a false statement.

		Answers		
1.	The ESC key is used to change the cursor from text-entry to move mode (Obj. 1)	1.	T	F
2.	When the cursor is in move mode, it displays the @ symbol (Obj. 1)......	2.	T	F
3.	To move the cursor 24 characters to the left with one command, strike the D key while in move mode (Obj. 1)	3.	T	F
4.	To move the cursor one character to the right, strike the K key while in move mode (Obj. 1)..........	4.	T	F
5.	To change the cursor from move mode to text-entry mode, either strike the space bar or press RETURN (Obj. 1)	5.	T	F
6.	The screen can display 24 lines of text at one time (Obj. 1)	6.	T	F
7.	Text that has scrolled off the screen is still in memory (Obj. 1)..........	7.	T	F
8.	The fastest way to move the cursor to the end of the text is to enter [*B*] (Obj. 1)	8.	T	F
9.	When [*E*] is entered, the direction arrow will point to the right (Obj. 1) ..	9.	T	F
10.	[*D*] can be entered to change the direction arrow (Obj. 2)..........	10.	T	F
11.	To insert text, position the cursor at the point where the text is to be inserted (Obj. 3)	11.	T	F
12.	To delete a character, position the cursor in front of the character to be deleted (Obj. 4)	12.	T	F

COMPLETION

For each of the following functions, write in the Keys column the key or combination of keys that should be used. Remember to put brackets around any control characters.

Function	Keys
1. Move the cursor left one character (Obj. 1)	1. ____________
2. Move the cursor up one line (Obj. 1)	2. ____________
3. Move the cursor down 12 lines (Obj. 1)..........	3. ____________
4. Move the cursor to the right 24 characters (Obj. 1)	4. ____________
5. Move the cursor down the screen rapidly (Obj. 1)........	5. ____________
6. Move the cursor to the beginning of the text (Obj. 1) ...	6. ____________
7. Move the cursor to the end of the text (Obj. 1)	7. ____________
8. Change the direction arrow (Obj. 2)..........	8. ____________

COMPUTER EXERCISE

In this Computer Exercise, you will load the file that was saved in Lesson 5. You will make changes in the file (including the correction of any errors you made before). You will then save the changed text and print the document. Follow these steps as you use the computer:

1. Load *Apple Writer.*
2. Display the student diskette catalog to verify the name of your text file.
3. Load your file from Lesson 5.
4. Practice moving the cursor using the I, J, K, and M keys.
5. Practice moving the cursor using the E, S, D, and X keys.
6. Practice moving the cursor using the [*B*] and [*E*] functions.
7. Change the text by making the corrections indicated on the next page. Also, correct any errors that you made in Lessons 4 and 5.

December 8, 19--

Dear Patricia,

It was great to receive a ~~holiday~~ note
from you and to hear you are doing well. We've really missed you since you
moved to WARM Florida. I know you're enjoying
the sunny shores at Ft. Lauderdale ~~Daytona~~.

Up here in snow country, we have almost
become accustomed to our annual blizzard. It
arrived with full fury last night and was it ever cold. We now
have almost three feet of snow on the ground!

Perhaps you can come up for a visit in
the summer. If you wait until it is warm, we
can go skiing on Lake George. Won't that be
great fun! Give me a call and let me know
when you can come. The boat and skiis are
waiting.

Cordially,

Erik

8. Save the text by entering [*S*] and =.
9. Print the text by entering [*P*] and *NP*.
10. When the printing is finished, quit *Apple Writer*, power down the computer, and remove your diskettes.

7. More Text-Editing Functions

OBJECTIVES:

1. Explain how to delete words using [*W*].
2. Explain how to delete paragraphs using [*X*].
3. Explain how to replace text using [*R*].
4. Give the procedure for moving text from one location to another.

CHANGING TEXT

In Lesson 6 you learned how to insert text. You also learned how to delete text using the backspace key. There are two additional ways to delete text which are faster than using the backspace key. A word or a paragraph may be deleted with a single command.

Deleting a Word

To delete a word, position the cursor immediately after the word to be deleted. The direction arrow on the Data Line must be pointing to the left (<). If it is not, enter [*D*]. Then enter [*W*] (for word). The word and the space before the word will be deleted. The computer always deletes the entire word and the space before it regardless of the length of the word. The computer knows the length of the word because the space before the word marks the beginning of it. To delete several words in a row, position the cursor to the right of the last word and enter [*W*] for each word to be deleted.

Deleting a Paragraph

Just as you can delete an entire word with one command, you can also delete an entire paragraph with one command. Position the cursor immediately after the paragraph you wish to delete. The direction arrow on the Data Line must be pointing to the left (<). If it is not, enter [*D*]. Then enter [*X*] to delete the paragraph. The computer knows where the paragraph to be deleted begins because it looks for the last place in the text where you pressed RETURN. This marks the end of the previous paragraph. To delete several paragraphs, position the cursor after the last paragraph and then enter [*X*] for each paragraph to be deleted.

Replacing Text

Text can be changed by replacing old text with new text. To do this, position the cursor at the beginning of the text to be replaced. Then enter [*R*] (for replace). Notice that an *R* is placed on the Data Line to remind you that you are in replace mode. In replace mode, each character that you enter replaces an old character. When you are finished replacing text, enter [*R*] again to return to regular text-entry mode.

MOVING TEXT

Use of the backspace key, [*W*], or [*X*] causes text to be deleted from the screen and from memory. However, text deleted in these ways is not immediately lost. Characters are temporarily saved in a **buffer**. A buffer is a temporary storage space reserved for text. It is not part of the memory space used for entering text. Text that you have deleted can be recalled from the buffer and reinserted into the text. This feature allows you to move text from one location in the file to another.

To move text using the backspace key, position the cursor to the right of the text that is to be moved. Delete the text. The maximum number of characters the buffer can store if you use this method is 128. After deleting the text to be moved, position the cursor at the point where the text is to be inserted. Strike the key with the arrow pointing right (→) until all of the text you deleted is inserted at the correct point. All remaining text will be shifted to the right and down to make room.

To move text using the [*W*] or [*X*] functions, position the cursor to the right of the text that is to be moved. The direction arrow should be pointing to the left (<). If it is not, enter [*D*]. Delete the text using either of the two deletion functions. The maximum number of characters the buffer can store when these functions are used is 1024. After deleting the text to be moved, position the cursor at the point where the text is to be inserted. Then change the direction arrow to the right (>) by entering [*D*]. Use the same function again that you used to delete. The text that you deleted will be inserted at this point and all remaining text will be shifted to the right and down to make room. In summary, you can conclude that the direction arrow on the Data Line works with [*W*] and [*X*] to either delete or insert text, depending on which direction the arrow points.

LESSON 7 EXERCISE Name ______________________ Date __________

TRUE/FALSE

Each of the following statements is either true or false. Indicate your choice in the Answers column by circling T for a true statement or F for a false statement.

	Answers		
1. To delete a word, you must position the cursor immediately before the word to be deleted (Obj. 1)	1.	T	F
2. [*X*] is entered for deleting one word (Obj. 1)	2.	T	F
3. For deletion to occur using any of the three functions, the direction arrow must point to the left (Objs. 1, 2)	3.	T	F
4. When you delete a word, the word and the space following the word are deleted at the same time (Obj. 1)	4.	T	F
5. If you want to delete several words in a row, you must position the cursor before the first word to be deleted (Obj. 1)	5.	T	F
6. The function that is used to delete an entire paragraph is [*X*] (Obj. 2) ...	6.	T	F
7. If you want to delete a paragraph, you should position the cursor immediately after the paragraph to be deleted (Obj. 2)	7.	T	F
8. The computer determines the length of a paragraph by looking for the last place in the text where you pressed RETURN (Obj. 2)	8.	T	F
9. Several paragraphs in a row can be deleted by positioning the cursor after the last paragraph to be deleted (Obj. 2)	9.	T	F
10. You use [*R*] to delete old text as you enter new text (Obj. 3)	10.	T	F
11. To leave the replace mode, you must enter [*R*] again (Obj. 3)	11.	T	F
12. A buffer is a temporary storage space in memory (Obj. 4)	12.	T	F
13. The maximum number of characters of text that can be moved using the [*W*] function is 128 (Obj. 4)	13.	T	F
14. Any of the three delete functions can be used to move text (Obj. 4)	14.	T	F
15. To insert text using [*W*], the direction arrow on the Data Line should point to the left (Obj. 4)	15.	T	F
16. When text is deleted, the remaining text is shifted up and to the left (Obj. 4)	16.	T	F

COMPLETION

For each of the following functions, write in the Keys column the key or combination of keys that should be used. Remember to put brackets around any control characters. Remember also that in some cases the direction arrow must be changed.

Function	Keys
1. To delete a word (Obj. 1)	1. ______________
2. To delete a paragraph (Obj. 2)	2. ______________

3. To replace text (Obj. 3) .... 3. ______________________
4. To return to regular text-entry mode from replace mode (Obj. 3) .... 4. ______________________
5. To prepare a paragraph to be moved (Obj. 4) .... 5. ______________________
6. To insert a word that has been moved (Obj. 4) .... 6. ______________________

COMPUTER EXERCISE

In this Computer Exercise, you will load the file from Lesson 6, make the indicated changes, then save and print the document. Follow the steps below as you use the computer:

1. Load *Apple Writer* and your file from Lesson 6.
2. Make the following changes using [*W*], [*X*], and [*R*]:

```
December [14] ~~8~~, 19--

Dear Patricia,

     It was great to receive a note from you
and to hear you are doing well.  We've really
missed you since you moved to ~~WARM Florida~~ [California].  I
know you're enjoying the [wonderful climate in] ~~sunny shores at~~
~~Ft. Lauderdale~~ [La Jolla].

[delete paragraph]
     Up here in snow country, we have almost
become accustomed to our annual blizzard.  It
arrived with full fury last night, and was it
ever cold.  We now have almost three feet of
snow on the ground!

     Perhaps you can come up for a visit in
the summer.  If you wait until it is warm, we
can go skiing on Lake George.  Won't that be
great fun!  Give me a call and let me know
when you can come.  The boat and skiis are
waiting.

Cordially,

Erik
```

3. Save the text by entering [*S*] and =.
4. Print the text by entering [*P*] and *NP*.
5. When the printing is finished, quit *Apple Writer*, power down the computer, and remove your diskettes.

8. Controlling Document Format

OBJECTIVES:

1. Give the procedure for setting selected print format values.
2. Explain how to save and load Print/Program Value Files.

The ability to edit text before it is printed is only one of the many features of a word processing system. After text has been entered and edited, the word processing operator can determine exactly how the printed document should appear.

SETTING PRINT VALUES

You have printed documents using the [*P*] and *NP* function in past lessons. When you printed the documents, you may have wondered how the computer knew what the left, right, top, and bottom margins should be. The computer uses values for these margins that are preset in the *Apple Writer* program. Preset values are called default values because when the *Apple Writer* program is loaded into the computer, these values are assigned automatically by the program.

These default values can be changed to produce different kinds of documents. To change the default values, enter [*P*] and then enter the question mark (*?*). The Print/Program Commands menu will appear on the screen as shown in Figure 8.1. This menu shows the various options for changing the format of a document. Next to each option is a two-letter code in parentheses followed by a number or two letters. These numbers or letters are the default values that are assigned when *Apple Writer* is loaded. Figure 8.2 explains each option.

Before changing these values, you should determine how many characters per horizontal inch and how many line spaces per vertical inch your printer produces. This information can be found in the printer manual. Computer printers usually print ten characters per horizontal inch (pica spacing) and six vertical lines to an inch. These values will be assumed in this lesson.

As an example, assume that you want to print a single-spaced document with top, bottom, left, and right margins of one inch. This requires six blank line spaces for both the top and bottom margins (6 line spaces = 1 inch). Therefore, you will set both the top and bottom margins to 6. The left margin will be set to 10 (10 horizontal spaces = 1 inch), and the right margin will be set to 75, since a sheet of 8 1/2-by-11-inch paper has 85 pica spaces.

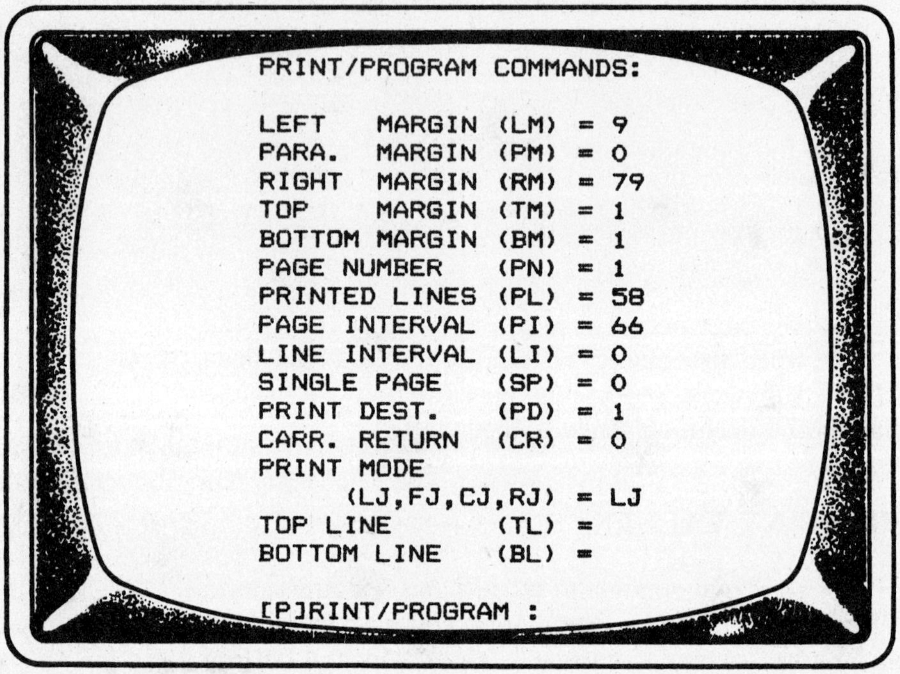

Figure 8.1 Print/Program Commands Menu

At the bottom of the Print/Program Commands menu you are prompted with *[P]rint/Program:* To set a new value, enter the two-letter code of the item you wish to change followed by the desired new value. For example, to set the left margin for one inch, enter *LM10.* The Print/Program Commands menu displays the value just entered. The prompt remains at the bottom of the screen, and another new value can be entered. The Print Mode is set by simply entering either *LJ, FJ, CJ,* or *RJ* instead of a number after *PM.*

After you have changed the format values, the document can be printed by entering *NP* in response to the *[P]rint/Program:* prompt. However, check first to make sure that the printer has been switched on and is ready to accept text for printing.

Left Margin (LM) = 9	Determines the left margin setting. The printing of each line begins at the specified number of spaces from the left edge of the paper.
Para. Margin (PM) = 0	Will be explained later.
Right Margin (RM) = 79	Determines the right margin setting. The printing of each line ends at the specified number of spaces from the left edge of the paper.
Top Margin (TM) = 1	Determines the number of blank lines between the top edge of the paper and the first printed line.
Bottom Margin (BM) = 1	Determines the number of blank lines between the last printed line and the bottom edge of the paper.
Page Number (PN) = 1	Will be explained later.
Printed Lines (PL) = 58	Will be explained later.
Page Interval (PI) = 66	Will be explained later.
Line Interval (LI) = 0	Determines the number of blank lines between printed lines. A 0 (zero) indicates single spacing, 1 indicates double spacing, 2 indicates triple spacing, and so on.
Single Page (SP) = 0	Used to indicate to the printer whether single-sheet paper or continuous-form paper is being used. If you enter a 1 for single-sheet paper, *Apple Writer* will prompt you to insert a new sheet of paper into the printer at the completion of each printed page. A 0 (zero) indicates continuous-form paper.
Print Dest. (PD) = 1	Indicates the computer slot into which the printer card is plugged. Your instructor will tell you if the value of 1 is correct. A value of 0 (zero) directs printing to the screen. (If zero is used, select 0 for LM and 39 for RM (79 if you have an 80-column card).)
Carr. Return (CR) = 0	Sends a signal to your printer to move the paper up one line. If your printer does not automatically do this each time it begins to print a new line, change this value to 1.
Print Mode (LJ,FJ,CJ,RJ) = LJ	Used to determine how your text will be printed. LJ means left justify, which produces an even left margin and an uneven right margin. FJ means fill justify, which produces both right and left margins that are even. CJ means center justify, which causes each line of text to be centered horizontally. RJ means right justify, which produces an even right margin and an uneven left margin.
Top Line (TL):	Will be explained later.
Bottom Line (BL):	Will be explained later.

Figure 8.2 Print Format Options and Default Values

PRINT/PROGRAM VALUE FILES

Once you have set new format values, you can save them on diskette in a Print/Program Value File for later use. This is desirable because the same format is usually used for similar jobs. For example, the same format is usually used for producing letters. If you do not save the values, you must reenter them each time they are to be used.

To save format values in a Print/Program Value File, the Data Line or the Editor Menu must be displayed. Enter [*Q*] to display the Additional Functions Menu, then select Option 4 (*Save Print/Program Value File*). The *Enter file name:* prompt will appear at the bottom of the screen. Enter an appropriate file name such as *report* or *letter*. The Print/Program Value File will be saved on the diskette. It will appear in the diskette catalog as *PRT.* followed by the name you assigned. For example, a Print/Program Value File that was assigned the name of *table* would appear in the diskette catalog as *B 003 PRT.TABLE.* The *B* indicates that the file is saved as a binary (computer language) file. The *003* indicates the physical length of the file.

To load a Print/Program Value File, enter [*Q*], then select Option 3 (*Load Print/Program Value File*). In response to the *Enter file name:* prompt at the bottom of the screen, enter the name you assigned to the file when it was saved.

LESSON 8 EXERCISE Name ______________________ Date ____________

TRUE/FALSE

Each of the following statements is either true or false. Indicate your choice in the Answers column by circling T for a true statement or F for a false statement.

	Answers		
1. Values that are set when *Apple Writer* is loaded are called default values (Obj. 1)	1.	T	F
2. To display the Print/Program Commands menu, you enter [*P*] and then enter *NP* (Obj. 1)	2.	T	F
3. Most computer printers use pica-size type; that is, they print 12 characters to a horizontal inch (Obj. 1)	3.	T	F
4. There are typically 6 line spaces to a vertical inch (Obj. 1)	4.	T	F
5. To set a 1 1/2-inch left margin when printing at 10 CPI, LM is set to 18 (Obj. 1)	5.	T	F
6. The value that you set for the right margin (RM) is the number of spaces from the left edge of the paper (Obj. 1)	6.	T	F
7. For a one-inch right margin on 8 1/2-by-11-inch paper when printing at 12 CPI, you should set RM to 75 (Obj. 1)	7.	T	F
8. LI should be set to 2 for double spacing (Obj. 1)	8.	T	F
9. TM should be set to 12 for a 1 1/2-inch top margin (Obj. 1)	9.	T	F
10. BM should be set to 6 for a one-inch bottom margin (Obj. 1)	10.	T	F
11. To save a Print/Program Value File, enter [*Q*], then select Option 4 (Obj. 2)	11.	T	F
12. When a Print/Program Value File is loaded, default values are replaced (Obj. 2)	12.	T	F
13. Formats for similar jobs should be saved in a Print/Program Value File (Obj. 2)	13.	T	F
14. In the diskette catalog, a Print/Program Value File is indicated by the letter *T* and the letters *PRT.* before the file name you assigned (Obj. 2)	14.	T	F

COMPLETION

For each of the following situations, write in the Keys column the keys that would be struck to set the print format values. (Obj. 1)

Settings	Keys
1. Set a 1 1/2-inch left margin when printing at 10 CPI	1. ______________
2. Set a one-inch right margin when printing at 10 CPI	2. ______________
3. Set double spacing	3. ______________
4. Produce copy that has even left and right margins	4. ______________

5. Set a top margin of 1 1/2 inches .... 5. ____________________
6. Set a bottom margin of 2 inches.......................... 6. ____________________
7. Set the value for continuous-form paper .... 7. ____________________
8. Set the value for even left and right margins........... 8. ____________________

COMPUTER EXERCISE

In this Computer Exercise, you will load your file from Lesson 7 and print it after setting different print format values. Follow the steps below as you use the computer:

1. Load *Apple Writer* and the file you saved in Lesson 7.
2. Enter [*P*] and then a question mark (*?*) to display the Print/Program Commands menu.
3. Set the following format values (remember that you do not key the equals sign):
   LM = 20
   RM = 65
   TM = 12
   BM = 6
   LI = 0
   SP (should be set to 1 if you are using single-sheet paper or 0 if you are using continuous-form paper)
   CR (check with your instructor)
   PM = LJ (should already be set from default values)
4. Press RETURN to return to your text. Then enter [*Q*] and select Option 4. In response to the prompt *Enter file name:*, enter *paragraph.* The computer will then return to the text.
5. Enter [*O*] and select Option 1 to display the diskette catalog. The Print/Program Value File should be listed as *B 003 PRT.PARAGRAPH.*
6. Press RETURN twice to return to the text.
7. Enter [*P*], a question mark (*?*), and *NP* to print your file.
8. After the document has been printed, enter [*P*], then a question mark.
9. Select the following values (remember that you do not key the equals sign):
   LM = 10
   RM = 75
   TM = 6
   LI = 1
   You need not change any of the other values.
10. Print the file again and compare the format with that of the first printing.
11. Return to the text and enter [*Q*], then select Option 3 to load the Print/Program Value File you saved in Step 4.

12. Return to the Print/Program Commands menu and observe that the values you saved in Step 4 are now loaded into the computer.
13. Print the file again. The third document should be the same as the first document.
14. Quit *Apple Writer* and power down the computer.

9. Diskette Filing Procedures

OBJECTIVES:

1. Explain how to assign diskette labels and text file names.
2. Explain how to prepare documents with diskette file notations.
3. Explain how to rename, lock, unlock, and delete text files.

One of the chief advantages of word processing is that a number of documents can be stored on one diskette. However, diskettes fill up very quickly in a busy office. When the number of diskettes that are used increases, it is advisable to organize the diskettes into a library. The diskette library must be organized in such a way that text previously saved can be easily retrieved.

DISKETTE LIBRARY ORGANIZATION

To organize a diskette library, diskettes must be labeled, and the text files on the diskettes must be named. Procedures for labeling diskettes and naming text files will be explained in the following sections.

Labeling Diskettes

One method of labeling diskettes for an office diskette library is to assign a letter and a number to each diskette, such as *S001.* The letter identifies the department, such as *S* for Sales, *A* for Accounting, or *L* for Legal. The letter is necessary so that diskettes are not mixed up when they are transported from one department to another. This is the method of labeling that will be used in this lesson.

Another way to label diskettes is to name each one according to the type of document stored on the diskette. For example, a diskette could be labeled *LETTERS 9/15/84 - 10/30/84.* This label would indicate that the diskette contained all the letters written between the given dates.

Assigning Text File Names

After you determine your method for labeling diskettes, you should assign names to the text file on the diskettes in an organized way. In these lessons, you have been using the lesson number followed by your name as the text file name. In a business office, the text file name should indicate either the addressee on the document or the type of document. The date on which the document was created should be included as part of the text file name. For example, a letter addressed to Ms. Maria Hernandez dated December 4, 1984 could be saved as *HERNANDEZ 120484*. A contract created on March 6, 1985 could be saved as *CONTRACT 030685*. Text files that are saved with meaningful file names such as these can be easily identified in the diskette catalog.

When text is saved on diskettes organized into a library, many offices find that it is no longer necessary to keep printed copies of documents on file. The diskette itself becomes the file. Its small size considerably reduces the amount of storage space required in an office. Using a paperless file, however, requires that each document have a file notation included on it when it is printed. This is necessary so that the text can be retrieved from the diskette at any time. A file notation includes the diskette label followed by the text file name. For example, *A248-CONTRACT052484* indicates a contract created on May 24, 1984 that is stored on an accounting department diskette. If the document is a letter or memorandum, only the diskette label is included in the file notation. The addressee and date on the letter are assumed to be the text file name. For example, *M255* indicates Diskette 255 in the marketing department.

The placement of the diskette file notation on a document depends on the type of document. If the document is a letter or memorandum, the file notation (which is the diskette label only) is usually placed immediately after the reference initials at the bottom of the letter, as in the example letter shown in Figure 9.1.

```
has been scheduled for April 4.  If this is not convenient for you,
please arrange a time with my secretary.

I look forward to meeting with you.  We can discuss the new
engineering designs at that time.

Sincerely



Rita Paulson, Director
Engineering Department

ks:E314
```

Diskette 314 in the Engineering Department

Figure 9.1 Letter with Diskette File Notation

If the document is not a letter or a memorandum, the diskette file notation, which includes the diskette label and the text file name, can be printed at the top right corner of the document, as in the example shown in Figure 9.2. Lesson 15 will give methods for printing diskette notations on documents by using *Apple Writer*.

Diskette 432 in the Legal Department

```
          Page 4          L432-CONTRACT071884
```

A contract entered July 18, 1984

```
party of the first part agrees to purchase from party of the
second part at the purchase price in effect at the time of the
sale according to the discount schedule attached as Exhibit A a
quantity not less than 400 units.  Taxes, insurance . . .
```

Figure 9.2 Contract with File Notation at Top Right Corner

DOS COMMANDS

Apple Writer includes commands that help in maintaining a diskette library. These commands are called DOS (Disk Operating System) Commands. Enter [*O*] to display the DOS Commands menu illustrated in Figure 9.3. You are already familiar with Option 1, which displays a diskette catalog. To select one of the other options, key the number of the option.

Renaming a File

Option 2 from the DOS Commands menu, *Rename File*, lets you change the name of an existing file. When this option is chosen, the prompt *Enter File Name:* is displayed. In response to the prompt, enter the file name which appears in the diskette catalog, a comma, and the new file name. For example, after the prompt you might enter *SMITH110284,SMITH110484*. The file name will be changed to reflect the new date of November 4, 1984. After renaming a file, you may select another option from the DOS Commands menu or press RETURN to return to text in memory.

Locking and Unlocking Files

Text files can be **locked**. This means that they can be protected so that they cannot be erased or permanently changed. To

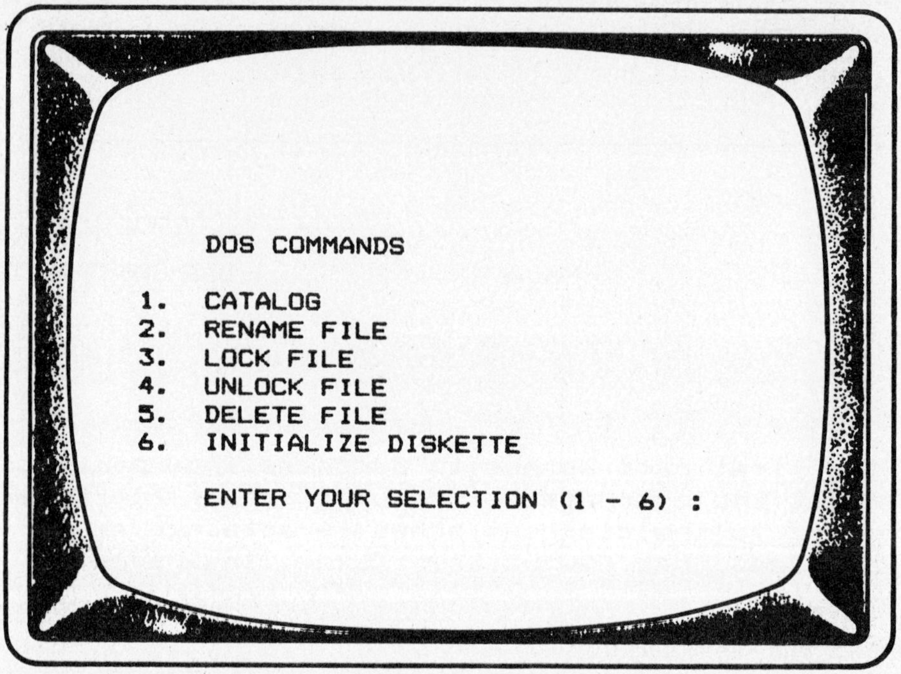

Figure 9.3 DOS Commands Menu

lock a text file, select Option 3 on the DOS Commands menu. In response to the *Enter File Name:* prompt, enter the name of the text file you wish to lock. The file will be locked immediately and an asterisk (*) will be displayed before that file name in the diskette catalog. When a text file is locked, it can still be loaded into memory, edited, and printed. However, it cannot be saved, renamed, or deleted (see the "Deleting Files" section below). To unlock a text file, select Option 4 from the DOS Commands menu. In response to the *Enter File Name:* prompt, enter the name of the text file you wish to unlock. The asterisk next to the file name in the diskette catalog is removed. The file is now unprotected, and it can be renamed, saved, or deleted. After locking or unlocking files, you may select another option from the DOS Commands menu, or press RETURN to return to your text.

Deleting Files

You should delete files that do not need to be permanently stored so that additional space can be made available on the diskette. Delete a file by selecting Option 5 from the DOS Commands menu. After the *Enter File Name:* prompt, enter the name of the file you want to delete. NOTE: Use this option carefully, because a file cannot be recovered after it has been deleted. If you attempt to delete a locked file, a warning tone will sound, and the message *DOS: File Locked* will be displayed. Respond to the prompt by pressing RETURN to return to the text in memory.

Initializing Diskettes

Option 6, *Initialize Diskette*, will be discussed in Lesson 12.

LESSON 9 EXERCISE Name ______________________ Date __________

TRUE/FALSE

Each of the following statements is either true or false. Indicate your choice in the Answers column by circling T for a true statement or F for a false statement.

		Answers		
1.	The letter in a diskette label (such as the *L* in L245) may indicate the department name (Obj. 1)	1.	T	F
2.	The date on which text is entered should be included in a text file name (Obj. 1)	2.	T	F
3.	A text file name for a letter would include the sender's name and the date the letter was sent (Obj. 1)..	3.	T	F
4.	The diskette file notation on a letter includes the diskette label and text file name (Obj. 2)	4.	T	F
5.	The diskette file notation on a letter should be placed in the top right corner (Obj. 2)	5.	T	F
6.	To rename a file, you enter the old file name, a comma, and the new file name. (Obj. 3)	6.	T	F
7.	Text files cannot be deleted while they are locked (Obj. 3)...............	7.	T	F
8.	Unlocked text files are indicated by an asterisk (*) in the diskette catalog (Obj. 3)	8.	T	F
9.	Locked text files cannot be printed (Obj. 3)	9.	T	F
10.	A file that has been deleted cannot be recovered (Obj. 3)	10.	T	F

COMPLETION

For each of the following functions, write in the Answers column the DOS Commands menu option that you would select, and the correct response to the *Enter File Name:* prompt. (Obj. 3)

Function	Answer
1. Change the name of a file from *JONES 041485* to *SMITH 041485*	1. ______________________
2. Protect a file named *CONTRACT*	2. ______________________
3. Prepare a locked file named *CHING030985* so that it can be renamed on the diskette	3. ______________________
4. Delete a file named *AGREEMENT 061985*	4. ______________________

COMPUTER EXERCISE

In this Computer Exercise, you will load the file that you saved in Lesson 8. You will make the indicated changes, and save the new version. Then you will print, lock, unlock, and delete the file.

1. Load *Apple Writer* and your file from Lesson 8.
2. Make the following changes:

```
          January 23
~~December 14~~, 19--

     Li-Ching
Dear ~~Patricia~~,

     It was great to receive a note from you
and to hear you are doing well.  We've really
                                St. Louis
missed you since you moved to ~~California~~.  ~~I~~
Have you visited the arch that is the gateway to the West?
~~know you're enjoying the wonderful climate in~~
~~La Jolla.~~

                                delete paragraph
     Perhaps you can come up for a visit in
the summer.  If you wait until it is warm, we
can go skiing on Lake George.  Won't that be
great fun!  Give me a call and let me know
when you can come.  The boat and skiis are
waiting.       I have enclosed some pictures that we took
               at your farewell party. You've never looked
               better than with the lampshade over your
Cordially,     head!! Write soon and tell me about St.
               Louis.

Erik
```

3. Save this new version with a file name of *LESSON 8* followed by your name.
4. Save the file again with the name of *EXAMPLE LESSON 8.*
5. Display the diskette catalog to see these two file names.
6. Print the file using the following format values. Remember that you do not key the equals sign.

LM = 15
RM = 70
TM = 6
BM = 6
LI = 0
SP (Set according to type of paper being used.)
CR (Set according to your printer.)
PM = LJ (This should already be set from default values.)

7. Change the *EXAMPLE LESSON 8* file name to your last name.
8. Lock the file that is titled with your last name.
9. Display the diskette catalog and check to see that the correct file has an asterisk, indicating that the file is locked.
10. Attempt to delete this file. You should hear a warning tone. The following message will be displayed: *DOS: File Locked.*
11. Unlock this file.
12. Delete the file.
13. Display the diskette catalog and check to see that the file is deleted.

NAME ______________________________ DATE ____________

10. Theory Test 1

In this lesson you will test your knowledge of the concepts and procedures you have learned in Lessons 1 through 9.

TRUE/FALSE

Each of the following statements is either true or false. Indicate your choice in the Answers column by circling T for a true statement or F for a false statement. NOTE: The objective number in parentheses following each question refers to the chapter number and corresponding objective number. For example, Obj. 1-1 indicates that the question was discussed in Chapter 1 and refers to the first objective in that chapter.

	Question	Answers		
1.	Word processing refers to using the computer to process text and produce documents (Obj. 1-1)	1.	T	F
2.	Groups of words are known as text (Obj. 1-1)	2.	T	F
3.	A document is printed from text (Obj. 1-1)	3.	T	F
4.	As you enter words into the computer, they are printed on paper by a printer (Obj. 1-1)	4.	T	F
5.	Diskettes are durable and require no special handling (Obj. 1-3)	5.	T	F
6.	*Apple Writer* is a group of instructions that makes the computer behave as a word processor (Obj. 1-4)	6.	T	F
7.	A control character is entered by keying a bracket, the character, and another bracket (Obj. 2-1)	7.	T	F
8.	Word wrap makes it unnecessary to press RETURN at the end of each line of a paragraph (Obj. 2-6)	8.	T	F
9.	To erase memory, select [*E*] (Obj. 2-2)	9.	T	F
10.	On the Data Line, *MEM: 18244* indicates the document in memory contains 18,244 characters (Obj. 2-3)	10.	T	F
11.	When the letter *Z* appears on the Data Line, word wrap is not engaged (Obj. 2-6)	11.	T	F
12.	You may not set tabs at column positions greater than 40 if the screen displays only 40 columns (Obj. 3-3)	12.	T	F
13.	To set or clear a tab stop, you should enter [*T*], which stands for tab (Obj. 3-3)	13.	T	F
14.	When the text for a document is stored on diskette, it is known as a file (Obj. 4-2)	14.	T	F

15. When you command the computer to save a file, the computer gets a name for the file from its catalog (Obj. 4-2) .... 15. **T** **F**
16. The command to save a file onto a diskette is [*F*] (for file) (Obj. 4-3)..... 16. **T** **F**
17. The diskette catalog is a list of the files stored on the diskette (Obj. 4-4) 17. **T** **F**
18. The diskette catalog is displayed by selecting [*Q*] (Obj. 4-4)........ 18. **T** **F**
19. If you cannot remember the name you used to save a file, it is impossible to load the file (Obj. 5-1) .... 19. **T** **F**
20. On most occasions, the computer's memory should be erased before loading a file (Obj. 5-1) .... 20. **T** **F**
21. If a file name is shown on the Data Line, the equals sign (=) may be used instead of the file name to resave the text under the name shown on the Data Line (Obj. 5-2) .... 21. **T** **F**
22. When [*P*] is entered, printing starts immediately (Obj. 5-3) .... 22. **T** **F**
23. Text that has scrolled off the screen is still in memory (Obj. 6-1)........ 23. **T** **F**
24. The fastest way to move the cursor to the end of the text is to enter [*B*] (Obj. 6-1) .... 24. **T** **F**
25. For deletion to occur using any of the three deletion functions, the direction arrow must point to the left (Obj. 6-4)........ 25. **T** **F**
26. When a whole word is deleted, the word and the space before the word are deleted (Obj. 7-1) .... 26. **T** **F**
27. To delete a paragraph, you should position the cursor immediately after the paragraph to be deleted (Obj. 7-2) .... 27. **T** **F**
28. Any of the three deletion functions can be used to move text (Obj. 7-4)... 28. **T** **F**
29. To insert text using [*W*] or [*X*], the direction arrow must point to the left (Obj. 7-4) .... 29. **T** **F**
30. To display the Print/Program Commands menu, enter [*P*] and then enter *NP* (Obj. 8-1) .... 30. **T** **F**
31. Most computer printers use pica-size type; that is, they print 12 characters to a horizontal inch (Obj. 8-1) .... 31. **T** **F**
32. Formats that can be used for similar jobs should be saved in a Print/Program Value File (Obj. 8-2) .... 32. **T** **F**
33. In the diskette catalog, a Print/Program Value File is indicated by the letter *T* and the letters *PRT* (Obj. 8-2)........ 33. **T** **F**
34. The date on which text is entered should be included in a text file name (Obj. 9-1) .... 34. **T** **F**
35. A text file name for a letter would include the sender's name (Obj. 9-1) 35. **T** **F**
36. The diskette file notation on a letter should be placed in the top right corner (Obj. 9-2) .... 36. **T** **F**
37. Text files cannot be deleted while they are locked (Obj. 9-3)........ 37. **T** **F**
38. A file that has been deleted cannot be recovered (Obj. 9-3) .... 38. **T** **F**

MATCHING

For each of the following, in the Answers column place the letter of the choice from Column 1 that best matches the phrase in Column 2.

Column 1	Column 2	Answers
A. [D]	39. Selecting the Additional Functions Menu (Obj. 1-5)	39. ________
B. [O] 1	40. Selecting the DOS Commands Menu (Obj. 4-4)	40. ________
C. [O]	41. Clearing all tab stops (Obj. 3-3).............................	41. ________
D. [Q]	42. Clearing one tab stop (Obj. 3-3).............................	42. ________
E. [X]	43. Displaying the diskette catalog (Obj. 4-4)	43. ________
F. [T] P	44. Erasing the computer's memory (Obj. 2-2)	44. ________
G. LI0	45. Changing the direction arrow (Obj. 6-2).....................	45. ________
H. [W]	46. Deleting a word (Obj. 7-1)	46. ________
I. LJ	47. Deleting a paragraph (Obj. 7-2)..............................	47. ________
J. [T] C	48. Replacing text (Obj. 7-3)....................................	48. ________
K. FJ	49. Setting double-spaced copy (Obj. 8-1)........................	49. ________
L. [S]	50. Setting copy that has even left and right margins (Obj. 8-1) . .	50. ________
M. LI1		
N. [N] Y		
O. [R]		

11. Skill Test 1

In this lesson you will demonstrate the text-editing skills you have learned in Lessons 1 through 9. Follow the steps below as you use the computer:

1. Load *Apple Writer* and enter the following text. Save the text with a file name of *LESSON 11 DRAFT* followed by your name.

```
THE WEEK'S HAPPENINGS, October 1-5

     Monday is a big day for the Drill Team.
Tryouts for next year will be held in the
gymnasium immediately after school.  Anyone
interested in trying out should sign up with
Miss Barrett no later than fifth period on
Monday.

     Also on Monday is the big magic show
sponsored by the Mighty Warrior Club.  The
Great Appleby will appear from 9:00 until
9:45.  Admission of one dollar must be paid
at the door.

     Students enrolled in information systems
classes will tour an airline reservations
center during fifth and sixth periods on
Thursday.  The bus will leave from the student
parking lot at 1:15.

     To bring the week to a grand finale, on
Friday night the Mighty Warriors will meet the
Wrightsburg Wildcats.  The Warriors are vowing
to continue their winning streak, which now
stands at four games.

xx:Cl
```

2. Print the file with the following format values: *LM 10, RM 75, TM 6, BM 6, LI 1.*
3. Assume that the printout from Step 2 has been edited as shown below. Make the changes on the computer. Then save the revised text under the file name *LESSON 11 DRAFT II* followed by your name.

```
THE WEEK'S HAPPENINGS, October 1-5

     Monday is a big day for the Drill Team.
Tryouts for next year will be held in the       Room 108
gymnasium immediately after school.  Anyone
interested in trying out should sign up with
Miss Barrett no later than fifth period on
Monday.
                                         Appleby has cancelled.
                                           Delete paragraph.
     Also on Monday is the big magic show
sponsored by the Mighty Warrior Club.  The
Great Appleby will appear from 9:00 until
9:45.  Admission of one dollar must be paid
at the door.

     Students enrolled in information systems
classes will tour an airline reservations
center during fifth and sixth periods on
Thursday.  The bus will leave from the student
parking lot at 1:15. Students will return to
school at 4:00 p.m.

     To bring the week to a grand finale, on
Friday night the Mighty Warriors will meet the
Wrightsburg Wildcats.  The Warriors are vowing
    extend
to continue their winning streak, which now
                     to five
stands at four games.

xx:Cl
```

4. Print the document again. For this printing, change the left margin to 15, the right margin to 70, and the line interval to 0 (zero).
5. Change the name of the file on disk from *LESSON 11 DRAFT II (your name)* to *LESSON 11 (your name)* and lock the file.
6. Delete the file named *LESSON 11 DRAFT (your name).*

12. Backup Procedures

OBJECTIVES

1. Give the reason for making backup copies.
2. Tell how to initialize a diskette.
3. Explain the procedure for making backup copies of individual files.
4. Tell how to copy an entire diskette.

Computers used for word processing are very reliable, as are the diskettes used for saving text. However, something may go wrong with the equipment from time to time. For this reason, you should always have more than one copy of important files. The copies should be on separate diskettes.

The copies you keep of files are known as **backup copies**. Backup copies can be made in two ways: The file can simply be saved on more than one diskette by using the *[S]ave:* command; or an exact duplicate can be made of an entire diskette by use of a special program provided with your computer. These two methods of making backup copies are discussed in the following sections. Since the methods may vary somewhat depending on whether you have one disk drive or two, be sure to follow the instructions for the number of drives in your computer system.

SAVING A FILE ON MORE THAN ONE DISKETTE

Any text that is in memory may be saved on any diskette. However, before a new diskette is used for the first time, it must be initialized. **Initialization** is a process that prepares the diskette to accept files. Until this is done, any attempt to save a file will be unsuccessful.

Initializing a Diskette

The steps in initializing a diskette were given in Lesson 1. However, if you did not initialize a diskette at that time, or if you need to review the process, it is presented here.

The first step in initializing a diskette is to power up the computer and load *Apple Writer*. Then insert the diskette that you want to initialize into Drive 2. If you have only one drive, remove the *Apple Writer* diskette and insert your new diskette into Drive 1.

WARNING: Initializing a diskette destroys any files that may already be recorded on the diskette. Therefore, never initialize your *Apple Writer* diskette or any other diskette that has valuable information stored on it.

Once you have inserted the new diskette into the disk drive, the initialization process is begun by choosing an option from *Apple Writer*'s DOS Commands menu. Remember from earlier lessons that this menu appears on the screen when you enter [*O*]. From the DOS Commands menu, select Option 6 (*Initialize diskette*). When you make this selection, a prompt is displayed at the bottom of the screen which reads *Enter Slot,Drive (Example S6,D1):* You must enter the drive number even if your computer has only one disk drive. You may omit the slot number. Therefore, if you want to initialize a diskette in Drive 1, enter either *S6,D1* or *D1*. To initialize a diskette in Drive 2, enter either *S6,D2* or *D2*.

When you press RETURN, the disk drive will run for about half a minute. When it stops, the diskette will be initialized, and the DOS Commands menu will reappear.

Copying An Individual File

A backup copy of a file can be made on any initialized diskette. In order to copy an individual file, power up the computer and load *Apple Writer*, then follow these steps:

1. If the file to be backed up is not already loaded, use [*L*] to load the desired file into memory from the student diskette.
2. Insert the diskette onto which the file is to be copied. This diskette is known as the backup diskette. If you have two disk drives, insert the backup diskette in Drive 2. If you have one disk drive, insert the backup diskette in Drive 1.
3. Use [*S*] to save the file onto the backup diskette. If you wish, you may use a different name for the backup copy than you used for the original file. Simply enter any file name you choose after the [*S*]*ave:* prompt. If the backup diskette is in Drive 2, remember to enter *,D2* after the file name.

DUPLICATING AN ENTIRE DISKETTE

If you want to duplicate an entire diskette, you may do so by using a special program supplied with your computer. This program automatically initializes the diskette before making the copy. Everything on the diskette is copied. Therefore, if any files are already on the backup diskette, they will be destroyed. To prevent accidental destruction of the original diskette, you should write-protect it before you duplicate it. To do this use a **write-protect tab**, which is a small piece of special adhesive paper. Do not use masking tape or any other kind of tape. Refer to Figure 12.1 and fold the tab around the edge of the diskette so that the write-protect notch is completely covered.

Figure 12.1 Write-Protect Tab on Diskette

To duplicate an entire diskette, you need the Apple system master diskette. If this diskette has not been supplied, ask your instructor for it. Make sure you have the Apple system master diskette, the diskette you want to duplicate, and a blank or out-of-date diskette on which to make the copy. Here are the steps to follow in making the copy:

1. If *Apple Writer* has been loaded, quit *Apple Writer* and remove the *Apple Writer* diskette.
2. Insert the Apple system master diskette into Drive 1. If the computer is turned off, power it up. If you are using an Apple IIe that is already powered up, hold down the CTRL key and the OPEN APPLE key (the apple picture key that is to the left of the space bar) while pressing the RESET key. If you are using an Apple II that is already powered up, enter *PR#6* (or the correct disk drive slot number for your computer).
3. When the disk drive stops running and the [(bracket) prompt appears on the screen, enter *RUN COPYA*. The disk drive will run briefly again. Then a series of prompts will be displayed. To understand these prompts, you need to know several terms: The original slot and drive are for the diskette being copied, and the duplicate

slot and drive are for the diskette onto which the copy is being made. If you have only one disk drive, the slot and drive numbers are the same for both the original and duplicate diskettes. Here are the prompts, with the correct responses shown:

```
APPLE DISKETTE DUPLICATION PROGRAM

  ORIGINAL SLOT:  DEFAULT = 6  <------ Press RETURN.

          DRIVE:  DEFAULT = 1  <------ Press RETURN.

 DUPLICATE SLOT:  DEFAULT = 6  <------ Press RETURN.

          DRIVE:  DEFAULT = 2  <------ Enter a 1 for a one-drive system,
                                       press RETURN for a two-drive system.
```

The prompt – *PRESS 'RETURN' KEY TO BEGIN COPY* – will be displayed. Before pressing RETURN, remove the Apple system master diskette and insert the original diskette into Drive 1. If you have two disk drives, insert the duplicate diskette into Drive 2. When you press RETURN using a two-drive system, the copying process will proceed automatically. When you press RETURN using a one-drive system, you will be prompted to insert the original diskette and again press RETURN. Since you will have already inserted the original, just press RETURN and the duplicating process will begin. While it is under way, you will be prompted periodically to change diskettes. In other words, you will exchange the original and duplicate diskettes several times during the copying process.

When the copying is completed, the copy program will display a prompt asking whether you want to make another copy. Answer this question with a Yes or a No as desired. Normally you will not want to make another copy.

If you want to do no further work after the copy is done, remove the diskettes and power down the computer. If you want to go back to *Apple Writer*, place the *Apple Writer* diskette in the disk drive and restart the computer. (Remember, if you are using an Apple IIe, hold down CTRL and OPEN APPLE while striking RESET. If you are using an Apple II, enter *PR#6* (or the correct disk drive slot number for your computer).) This will reload *Apple Writer*.

In all future lessons, you should make a backup copy of each file that you create.

LESSON 12 EXERCISE Name ______________________ Date ____________

TRUE/FALSE

Each of the following statements is either true or false. Indicate your choice in the Answers column by circling T for a true statement or F for a false statement.

	Answers
1. Computers used for word processing are very reliable. Therefore, duplicate copies of important files are not needed (Obj. 1)	1. **T** **F**
2. Backup copies of files are usually kept on the same diskette as the original files (Obj. 1)	2. **T** **F**
3. New diskettes must be initialized before their first use (Obj. 2)	3. **T** **F**
4. Initializing a diskette erases everything that may have been saved on the diskette (Obj. 2)	4. **T** **F**
5. The option for disk initialization is selected from the DOS Commands menu (Obj. 2)	5. **T** **F**
6. Even if your computer has two disk drives, diskettes must be initialized in Drive 1 (Obj. 2)	6. **T** **F**
7. Any initialized diskette may be used to make a copy of an individual file (Obj. 3)	7. **T** **F**
8. When saving a file onto a backup diskette, the original and backup diskettes must both be in disk drives at the same time (Obj. 3)	8. **T** **F**
9. Saving a backup file can be done with one disk drive. However, to duplicate an entire diskette, two disk drives are necessary (Obj. 3)	9. **T** **F**
10. The option to duplicate an entire diskette is selected from *Apple Writer*'s DOS Commands menu (Obj. 4)	10. **T** **F**
11. To save a backup copy of a file, you must use a program on the Apple system master diskette (Obj. 4)	11. **T** **F**
12. The process for making a duplicate diskette is identical regardless of whether you are using one or two disk drives (Obj. 4)	12. **T** **F**

SEQUENCING

For each question, indicate the proper order of the listed operations by writing a number on each answer line. Write a 1 beside the operation that should be done first, a 2 beside the operation that should be done second, and so on.

1. What is the proper order of the steps to initialize a diskette? (Obj. 2)

______ Select Option 6 (Initialize diskette) from the *Apple Writer* DOS Commands menu.

______ Make sure the diskette you are about to initialize contains no valuable information.

______ Insert the diskette to be initialized into the disk drive.

______ Enter the slot and drive numbers.

2. What is the proper order for saving an individual file onto another diskette? (Obj. 3)

_______ Use the [*S*]*ave:* command to save the file.

_______ If the file is not already in the computer's memory, load it by entering [*L*].

_______ Make sure the backup diskette is in the disk drive.

3. What is the proper order for duplicating an entire diskette? (Obj. 4)

_______ Quit *Apple Writer* if it is loaded.

_______ Exchange diskettes as prompted by the program (if you are using one disk drive).

_______ Insert the Apple system master diskette and restart the computer.

_______ Insert the original diskette (and the duplicate diskette if you are using two disk drives).

_______ Enter *RUN COPYA.*

COMPUTER EXERCISE

In this Computer Exercise, you will initialize a diskette and make a backup copy of an individual file. You will also duplicate an entire diskette. You will need the *Apple Writer* diskette, the Apple system master diskette, and two blank or out-of-date diskettes. If all of these diskettes have not been made available to you, ask your instructor for them. Refer to the instructions in the lesson as you follow these steps:

1. Initialize one of the blank or out-of-date diskettes. Use a soft-tip pen to label this diskette with your name and the title DISK B.
2. From your student diskette, load the file you saved in Lesson 8. Insert Disk B (the diskette you initialized in Step 1 above). Save the file onto Disk B under the name *LESSON 12 (your initials).* Display the diskette catalog of Disk B to verify that the file was saved.
3. From your student diskette, load the file you saved in Lesson 8. Use the same name to save the file onto Disk B. Display the diskette catalog to verify that the file was saved.
4. Using the *COPYA* program, make a duplicate of Disk B. After making the duplicate, display the diskette catalog for both Disk B and the duplicate. Note that the catalogs are identical. Label the duplicate diskette with your name and the title *DISK C.*

13. Producing a Simple Report

OBJECTIVES:

1. Describe the format for a report.
2. Explain how to calculate margin settings.
3. Explain how to set up *Apple Writer* for printing a report.
4. Explain how to enter, save, and print a report.

The name **report** is given to a wide variety of documents. In general, all reports present information to the reader in paragraph form. Some examples of reports are book reports and term papers. Figure 13.1 shows the first page of a typical report.

REPORT FORM

By setting up a report as suggested in this lesson, you will have a document that looks professional and is easy to read. Reports that look professional improve your image in the eyes of the reader, whether the reader is a teacher or your employer. A report represents the person who prepares it.

Print Sizes

Some of the information you give *Apple Writer* about a report format will vary depending on the print size you are using. Since print sizes differ with each type of printer, check with your instructor about the print sizes available on your printer.

Two common print sizes are 10 CPI (characters per inch) and 12 CPI. Multiplying the standard paper width (8.5 inches) by the number of characters in an inch gives the number of available print columns on the paper. At 10 CPI there are 85 available columns. At 12 CPI there are 102 available columns.

Margins

The space between the edge of the paper and the printed words is known as a margin. Therefore, a report has a left margin, a right margin, a top margin, and a bottom margin. The left margin of an unbound report should be one inch. Therefore, the left margin setting should be the number of characters in one inch (10 or 12).

ELECTRONIC TYPESETTING

Probably no development since the invention of moveable type has had as much impact on the printing industry as has electronic typesetting. It is a technology that has made itself felt from the smallest neighborhood printshop to the largest corporate giant.

The earlier electronic typesetters (or composers, as they are called) required that all text be entered on their keyboards. In other words, it mattered not whether an author had composed a document using pencil and paper, typewriter, or word processor. To typeset the material, the text had to be rekeyed on the typesetter's own keyboard.

Persistent developments, however, led first to a unit capable of receiving text over a phone line from a computer or word processor. Then units were developed to read the floppy disks produced by a multitude of computers and word processors directly. Since direct reading is much faster than communicating over a phone line, the text is made available to the composer much more quickly.

Once the reading of text is complete, the codes used by the originating word processor for underlining, bold printing, and so on, are automatically translated to the codes required internally by the composer.

Figure 13.1 Report Format (Shown Printed at 10 CPI)

For the right margin setting, subtract the number of characters in an inch from the number of columns available across the page. At 10 CPI, subtract 10 from 85, which gives a margin setting of 75. At 12 CPI, subtract 12 from 102, which gives a margin setting of 90.

The top margin of the first page of a report is usually 1.5 inches at 10 CPI. Multiply 1.5 times 6 (the number of lines in an inch) to get a margin of 9 lines, with printing beginning on Line 10. At 12 CPI, the top margin of the first page is usually 2 inches. Multiply 2 times 6 to get a margin of 12 lines, with printing beginning on Line 13. For convenience when adding additional pages to a report (as you will do in Lesson 14), it is recommended that the top margin be set to one inch. Then press RETURN either three times or six times to get the desired first page margin.

The bottom margin should be 1 inch, which is 6 blank lines. When text requires less than a full page, however, the bottom margin will be larger.

Spacing

The number of blank lines between lines of print is known as the **line interval**. After the heading of a report, there are two blank lines (a line interval of two). Other lines have a line interval of one; that is, there is one blank line between each pair of printed lines. Refer again to Figure 13.1 to see the spacing of a simple report.

Printed Lines

Most printers print six lines per inch. Therefore, if you are printing on standard 11 inch paper, you would suspect that the maximum number of printed lines on a page is 66 (6 lines times 11 inches). With *Apple Writer*, this may or may not be true. If you want to, you can specify a maximum number of printed lines less than the physical length of the paper. For this lesson, however, you should specify 66 printed lines per page.

Heading

The **heading** of a report is its title. It tells what the report is about. The heading, in uppercase letters, is centered on the first line below the top margin. Refer again to Figure 13.1 to see the placement of the heading.

Justification

Justification refers to how lines of text are positioned on the page. *Apple Writer* gives you the choice of four kinds of justification. Center justification places each line of text in the horizontal center of the page, resulting in both left and right ragged (uneven) edges. Left justification starts all lines evenly at the left margin and leaves the right margin ragged. Right justification ends all lines evenly at the right margin, resulting in a ragged left margin. Fill justification inserts extra spaces between words so that all lines start evenly at the left margin and end evenly at the right margin. In Figure 13.1, the heading is center justified. All other lines of text are left justified.

CONTROLLING *APPLE WRITER*'S PRINT FORMAT

There are two methods of controlling *Apple Writer*'s print format. As you learned in Lesson 8, one of these is the use of the Print/Program Commands menu. The other is the use of text-embedded print commands.

Using the Print/Program Commands Menu

In this lesson, you will use the Print/Program Commands menu to set the margins and the line spacing. Remember that this menu is selected by entering [*P*]. When the [*P*]*rint/Program:* prompt appears at the bottom of the screen, enter a question mark (*?*) to display the format options. Then enter the new values. If necessary, review the steps given in Lesson 8. Here are the values to enter for a report, for both 10 CPI and 12 CPI:

Command	10 CPI	12 CPI
LM (Left Margin)	10	12
RM (Right Margin)	75	90
TM (Top Margin)	6	6
BM (Bottom Margin)	6	6
PL (Printed Lines)	66	66
LI (Line Interval)	0	0

Remember that once the settings have been made, they may be saved on the diskette for future use. To do this, enter [*Q*] to display the Additional Functions Menu. Then select Option 4 (*Save Print/Program Value File*) and enter a file name under which the values will be stored.

Using Text-Embedded Print Commands

Any print commands that may be entered with the Print/Program Commands menu may also be placed in your text. Print commands that are placed in your text are called **embedded** print commands. *Apple Writer* always begins printing by using the values from the Print/Program Value File. Then whenever it finds a value embedded in the text, it changes to the embedded value. This feature makes it easy to have a two-inch top margin on the first page and a one-inch top margin on other pages.

Each print command to be embedded in the text is entered on

a separate line, with a RETURN both before and after the line. Enter a period, then the two-letter command abbreviation and the setting. Here are two examples: *.CJ* tells the computer to center justify the following text; and *.FJ* tells the computer to align the following text at left and right margins.

When you enter the text for this lesson's computer exercise, you will use some text-embedded print commands. The heading will be center justified, while the other lines will be left justified. Here is how the first several lines you enter should look. *(RETURN)* is used to show you where to press RETURN.

(RETURN) (RETURN) (RETURN)	Since top margin is set to six, these RETURNS will make 1.5-inch top margin on first page
.CJ (RETURN)	Center justify heading
ELECTRONIC TYPESETTING (RETURN)	Heading of report in uppercase letters
.LJ (RETURN)	Left justify rest of text
(RETURN) (RETURN)	First and second blank lines after heading
.LI1	Set line interval to 1 for remainder of report

UNDERLINING

Another text-embedded command that can be used causes text to be underlined when it is printed. (Some printers cannot underline, so this command may not work on your printer.) Text to be underlined is marked by a reverse slash (\) at the beginning and end. (If you are using an Apple II, enter the reverse slash by striking ESC and then holding down the SHIFT and CTRL keys while striking *P*.) Put the slashes where the spaces between words normally go. For example, the line *THE\FIRST WORDS\I HAVE UNDERLINED* will be printed as *THE FIRST WORDS I HAVE UNDERLINED.*

Notice in the preceding example that the space between the words is not underlined. If you want the underline to continue between words, you must key it when entering the words. If you are using an Apple II, enter the underline by holding down the SHIFT and CTRL keys while striking *M*. For example *THE\FIRST_WORDS\I HAVE UNDERLINED* will be printed as *THE FIRST WORDS I HAVE UNDERLINED.* Remember: Once underlining starts, it will continue until the second reverse slash is found to end it. Therefore, if you forget to insert the second reverse slash, underlining will continue until the end of your document.

LESSON 13 EXERCISE Name ______________________ Date __________

TRUE/FALSE

Each of the following statements is either true or false. Indicate your choice in the Answers column by circling T for a true statement or F for a false statement.

		Answers		
1.	A business letter is a typical report (Obj. 1)	1.	T	F
2.	The space between the edge of the paper and the printed words is known as a margin (Obj. 2)	2.	T	F
3.	The top margin on the first page of a report is usually one inch (Obj. 2)	3.	T	F
4.	The right and left margins of an unbound report are the same size (Obj. 2)	4.	T	F
5.	The lines of a report usually have a line interval of one (Obj. 1)	5.	T	F
6.	The heading of a report usually begins at the left margin (Obj. 1)	6.	T	F
7.	Right justification causes all lines to begin at the left margin and end evenly at the right margin (Obj. 1)	7.	T	F
8.	Fill justification creates even left and right margins (Obj. 1)	8.	T	F
9.	*Apple Writer* can center lines for you (Obj. 3)	9.	T	F
10.	Print formats can be controlled from the Print/Program Commands menu (Obj. 3)	10.	T	F
11.	Text-embedded print commands become effective when they are found by *Apple Writer* as it prints text (Obj. 3)	11.	T	F
12.	By using reverse slashes, you can cause *Apple Writer* to underline words (Obj. 3)	12.	T	F

COMPLETION

1. On the lines below, enter the requested information for each margin of a report. (Obj. 2)

Margin	Size (In Inches)	Settings: 10 CPI	Settings: 12 CPI	Settings: Lines
a. Left Margin	________	_____	_____	
b. Right Margin	________	_____	_____	
c. Top Margin (after page 1)	________			_____
d. Bottom Margin	________			_____

2. On the lines below, enter the correct *Apple Writer* command from the Print/Program Commands menu for making the following settings. Be sure to include the codes for the commands and the values, if any, that follow them. (Obj. 3)

Settings	Command/Value
a. Set left margin to 10	a. ________
b. Set right margin to 75	b. ________
c. Set top margin to one inch	c. ________

d. Set bottom margin to one inch .... d. ____________

e. Set a line interval of one .... e. ____________

f. Set to center justify .... f. ____________

g. Set to left justify .... g. ____________

h. Set to fill justify................................ h. ____________

3. Describe how to underline words. (Obj. 3) ____

____

____

COMPUTER EXERCISE

In this Computer Exercise, you will enter a one-page report, save it, and print it in the correct format.

1. Enter the partial report shown in Figure 13.1. Use text-embedded print commands for centering the heading, setting up left justification, and setting the line interval. Don't forget to use the reverse slashes for underlining. When you have entered the report, save your text on the student diskette.
2. Select the Print/Program Commands menu and enter the values given in this lesson to set up the format for printing a report. Then select Option 4 from the Additional Functions Menu, and save the Print/Program values in a file named *REPORT FORMAT*.
3. Print the report. The file that you create in this lesson will be used again in Lesson 14, so do not delete it from the diskette.

14. Producing a Two-Page Report with a Footnote

OBJECTIVES:

1. Describe the format for the second and succeeding pages of a report.
2. Describe the use of a top-line entry and footnotes in a report.
3. Explain *Apple Writer*'s procedures for printing top-line entries and footnotes.
4. Explain how to create, save, and print a two-page report that has a top-line entry and footnotes.

In Lesson 13 you entered and printed a simple report. In this lesson you will prepare a more complex two-page report.

ADDITIONAL REPORT FEATURES

Some additional features of a report's format concern page numbers, the margins, and footnotes. As you study these features in the following paragraphs, refer to Figure 14.1 for an illustration.

Page Numbers

When a report has several pages, the pages should be numbered. The page number is usually placed at the top right or bottom center of the page. The number on the first page may be omitted, if desired. Other identifying information such as the date may be placed on the same line as the page number.

Margins

Remember that the top margin on the first page of a report may be either 1.5 inches or 2 inches. On pages after the first, the top margin is only 1 inch. The side and bottom margins remain the same as on the first page.

Footnotes

Any page of a report, including the first one, may contain one or more footnotes. Footnotes give the sources of the writer's information or provide additional explanations of the topic. A **superscript** (number raised slightly above the line) is used to indicate each footnote reference. The same superscript and the footnote are then printed at the bottom of the page on which the reference appears. A 1.5-inch-long line separates the body of the report from the footnotes.

January 21, 1985 Typesetting Report 2

The translation process can also set up special codes required for changing type styles and sizes. For example, translation can be set up so that the entry <intro> is changed to the codes telling the composer to use a predetermined size, style, and format for the introduction of a book.(1)

Once the translation process is complete, the finished document is displayed on a CRT. On the screen, all headings are in the proper size and type style. Also, all text material is displayed just as it will be typeset. If changes are desired, they are easily made. For example, the type size for headings might be increased or the margins changed. Once the user is satisfied with the appearance of the document, only a few keystrokes are required to accomplish the actual typesetting for printing.

For any business that prints reports, articles, or books, the computer-controlled typesetter provides many benefits. Work can be done faster, more professionally, and at lower cost.

----

(1)William W. Maxey, Printing Technology (Atlanta: Eagle Press, 1983), p. 112.

Figure 14.1 Second Page of a Report Showing Top-Line Entry and Footnote

USING *APPLE WRITER* FOR A MORE COMPLEX REPORT

If a report has footnotes, top-line entries, or bottom-line entries, there are special procedures that must be used to prepare the text for printing. These procedures are discussed in the following paragraphs.

Top-Line Entries

Apple-Writer's top-line entry or bottom-line entry feature is used to print page numbers and any other desired information at the top or bottom of each page. For example, the text in Figure 14.1, which is the second page of the report you began in the last lesson, has the following line at the top of the page:

```
January 21, 1985          Typesetting Report          2
```

You can specify up to three items to be printed. The first item starts at the left margin, the second item is centered, and the third item ends at the right margin.

The methods you use to make a top-line entry and bottom-line entry are almost identical. The only difference is that the top-line entry is set by using the initials *TL*, while the bottom-line entry is set by using the initials *BL*. The following instructions refer only to top-line entry. However, substituting *BL* for *TL* makes them work for bottom-line entry.

A top-line entry can be entered as a code on the Print/Program Commands menu. However, it is recommended that you enter it as a text-embedded command. This has two advantages: (1) It enables you to begin the top-line entry on the second page rather than the first, giving a better appearance to the first page; and (2) The Print/Program file should contain a format that is appropriate for any report, rather than a format that is usable by just one. To cause a top-line entry to be printed beginning on the second page, the text-embedded command for the entry may appear anywhere at or near the beginning of the text. The entry will be printed for the first time at the top of the next page after its entry in the text.

To put a top-line entry in your text, first move the cursor to the place you want to put the text-embedded command, probably at the beginning of your text. Then decide on some character you will use to separate the three possible print items from each other. This character is known as a **delimiter**. Any character other than the reverse slash (\) and the number sign (#) may be used. Key *.TL* at the left edge of the screen (be sure you position the cursor at the left edge of the screen by pressing RETURN). After the *.TL* on the screen (no space), key the delimiter character you have chosen, followed by the item you want printed at the left side of the paper. Key the delimiter again, followed by the item you want printed in the center of the paper. Key another delimiter character, then the item to appear at the right side of the paper, and a final delimiter character. Put a number sign (#) between the delimiters at whatever point you want the page number to be printed. Here are two examples, both using the asterisk (*) as the delimiter:

Title will print at center of page.

```
.TL*JANUARY 21, 1985*TYPESETTING REPORT*#* (RETURN)
```

Date will print at left edge of page.

Page number will print at right edge of page.

Page number will print at right edge of page.

```
.TL***#* (RETURN)
```

Nothing between first two sets of delimiters means nothing will print in the left and center positions.

Footnotes

Apple Writer will automatically place footnotes at the end of the page containing their references. However, it will not print a line to separate the body of the report from the footnotes. The procedure that you use to enter a footnote consists of two steps: The first step is to enter the reference number in the text, and the second step is to enter the footnote itself immediately following the reference.

If your printer cannot make superscripts, you may place the reference number in parentheses. However, most daisy wheel printers and many dot matrix printers can make superscripts. If your printer can make superscripts, you should indicate that the footnote reference number should be raised slightly above the normal print line. The printer does this by moving the paper down slightly, printing the number, then moving the paper back to its normal position. To make the printer behave this way, you must know the proper commands. Some daisy wheel printers, for example, require an *ESC SHIFT-D* to move the paper down a fraction of a line (the *D* stands for down) and an *ESC SHIFT-U* (the *U* stands for up) to move the paper back to its normal position. (Note that you do not spell out the commands. *ESC SHIFT-D*, for example, means that you strike the ESC key, then hold down the SHIFT key while striking the *D* key. Nothing appears on the screen when you strike the ESC key.) Check with your instructor or refer to the printer's instruction manual to get the commands for your printer.

Superscripts
Subscripts

Once you know the required commands, place them between two [*V*]s in your text at the point where the footnote reference number should appear. Any characters placed between [*V*] and [*V*] will be sent to the printer as commands rather than as characters to be printed on the paper. Using the footnote reference from Figure 14.1 and the sample printer code from the last paragraph as an example, here is how you would enter text to make the superscript:

Moves paper down a fraction of a line

```
style, and format.[V]ESC SHIFT-D[V]1[V]ESC SHIFT-U[V]
```

Prints reference number

Moves paper back up to normal position

After entering the reference number, you should immediately enter the footnote. Do not try to place it at the end of the page yourself. So that *Apple Writer* will know it is a footnote, put a (< at the beginning and a >) at the end of each line. You must determine where each line of the footnote should end; *Apple Writer*'s right margin does not function for footnotes. If your printer can make a superscript for the footnote number, remember to include the necessary code at the beginning of the footnote. Also, remember to enter the 1.5-inch separator line above the first footnote on a page. Here is an example, showing how the footnote for Figure 14.1 may be entered:

```
(<__________________>)
(< >)
(<[V]ESC SHIFT-D[V]1[V]ESC SHIFT-U[V]William M. Maxey,\Printing
Technology\(Atlanta:  Eagle>)
(<Press, 1983), p. 112.>)
```

When the document is printed, *Apple Writer* will automatically move the footnote to the bottom of the page.

To ensure that a footnote appearing on the last page of the report will be printed, you should tell *Apple Writer* to feed out the last page. After pressing RETURN at the end of the last sentence of your report, key *.FF* (for form feed) at the left edge of the screen, but do not press RETURN afterwards. Pressing RETURN will cause the top-line entry (if any) to be printed at the top of a blank page after the end of your text.

Controlling Margins when Using Top-Line or Bottom-Line Entries

When *Apple Writer* prints top-line entries or bottom-line entries, it places these entries on the first available print lines at the top or bottom of the page. Remember that in Lesson 13 we specified that the number of printed lines (PL) on the page was 66, with a top margin (TM) of 6 lines and a bottom margin (BM) of 6 lines. Using these settings, *Apple Writer* would place a top-line entry on the very first line of the page, with 6 blank lines between the top-line entry and the first line of your text. It would place a bottom-line entry on the very last line of the page, with 6 blank lines between the last line of text and the bottom-line entry. This would not be the best placement for a top-line entry or bottom-line entry. To correct this problem, the number of printed lines (PL) must be changed. The desired placement for top-line and bottom-line entries is one-half inch (3 lines) from the top and bottom of the paper. This can be done by setting PL to 60. The top and bottom margins must be changed to 2 (the number of blank lines that usually looks best between the top and bottom entries and your text). You will then have to manually turn the paper to the fourth line before turning on the printer. The printing of the top-line entry will thus begin one-half inch from the top of the page.

LESSON 14 EXERCISE Name ______________________________ Date ____________

TRUE/FALSE

Each of the following statements is either true or false. Indicate your choice in the Answers column by circling T for a true statement or F for a false statement.

		Answers
1.	The top margin on the second page of a report is one inch (Obj. 1)	1. T F
2.	Footnotes may not be placed on the first page of a report (Obj. 1)	2. T F
3.	A page number always appears at the bottom of a page (Obj. 1)	3. T F
4.	The top-line entry on a report may contain information other than the page number (Obj. 2)	4. T F
5.	A footnote may be used to refer the reader to a source of information (Obj. 2)	5. T F
6.	*Apple Writer*'s top-line entry feature allows the printing of up to three different items at the top of each page (Obj. 3)	6. T F
7.	Either the Print/Program Commands menu or text-embedded commands may be used for printing a top-line entry (Obj. 3)	7. T F
8.	*Apple Writer* makes superscripts (Obj. 3)	8. T F
9.	*Apple Writer* automatically places footnotes at the bottom of the page on which they are entered (Obj. 3)	9. T F
10.	When using *Apple Writer*, you should enter a footnote immediately following its reference in the text (Obj. 3)	10. T F

COMPLETION

Write on each line provided the correct sequence of commands and words that would result in the specified part of a report.

1. Print a top-line entry with the date of *January 21, 19–* at the left, the words *DAILY REPORT* in the center, and the page number at the right. (Obj. 3) ______________________

   ____

2. Print a top-line entry with the date of *January 21, 19–* at the left and the page number at the right. (Obj. 3) ______________________

3. Print a top-line entry with the page number at the right. (Obj. 3) ______________________

4. Print a top-line entry with the page number in the center. (Obj. 3) ______________________

5. Print the reference in the text to Footnote 1 (use a superscript). (Obj. 3) ______________________

6. Enter the following footnote in the text as Footnote 1 (remember to enter a superscript): Pat Painter, <u>Looking Without Seeing</u> (Cheyenne: Mountain Press, 1982), p. 23. (Be sure to include the necessary characters to show it is a footnote.) (Obj. 3) ______________________

   ____

   ____

   ____

COMPUTER EXERCISE

For this Computer Exercise you will add a second page to the report that you created in Lesson 13. Perform the following steps:

1. Load the report that you created in Lesson 13.
2. Add the text and footnote from Figure 14.1. Insert a text-embedded print command at the beginning of the first page of text to set up the top-line heading. Enter the footnote immediately after its reference.
3. Save the updated text.
4. Load the Print/Program Value File created in Lesson 13 and saved under the name *REPORT FORMAT*. Do this by entering [*Q*] and selecting Option 3, *Load Print/Program Value File*. Enter new values for PL, TM, and BM as explained on page 104.
5. Print the report. The margins and line interval will be set automatically from the file you loaded in Step 4. The text-embedded command will set up the top-line entry beginning on page 2.

15. Producing a Report with a Long Quotation

OBJECTIVES:

1. Describe the format of a long quotation in a report.
2. Explain the procedure for changing margins during printing.
3. Explain how to change the line interval during printing.
4. Explain how to print a diskette notation at the bottom of each page of a report by using a bottom-line entry.
5. Explain the procedure for adding a long quotation and diskette notation to a report and printing the resulting report.

This is the last lesson in which you will learn about entering and printing a report. After completing it, you will be ready to handle almost any report that may be required.

THE FINAL TOUCHES

There are two more features of report format you need to know about in order to do a good job producing reports. They are the use of long quotations and the use of diskette notations. Refer to Figure 15.1 as you study the following paragraphs.

Long Quotations

Long quotations (those longer than two or three lines) are usually indented on both sides. To make the indention, the left and right margins are both temporarily moved five spaces toward the center. For example, if the left margin is set at 10, it is changed to 15. If the right margin is set at 75, it is changed to 70. After the long quotation is printed, the margins are returned to their original values. In addition to being indented, long quotations are also printed with a line interval of zero (single spacing). Long quotations are much easier to recognize when these two format changes are made.

Diskette Notations

If changes are to be made in a report after it has been saved on diskette, it is necessary to know where the report is stored.

January 21, 1985 Typesetting Report 2

The translation process can also set up special codes required for changing type styles and sizes. For example, translation can be set up so that the entry <intro> is changed to the codes telling the composer to use a predetermined size, style, and format for the introduction of a book. According to Maxey, this has great impact:

> The translation of word processor codes to those required by typesetting equipment has the potential of producing the greatest change ever seen in the printing industry. Its impact has already been felt and will be felt to a much greater extent than anyone would have imagined just a few years ago.(1)

Once the translation process is complete, the finished document is displayed on a CRT. On the screen, all headings are in the proper size and type style. Also, all text material is displayed just as it will be typeset. If changes are desired, they are easily made. For example, the type size for headings might be increased or the margins changed. Once the user is satisfied with the appearance of the document, only a few keystrokes are required to accomplish the actual typesetting for printing.

For any business that prints reports, articles, or books, the computer-controlled typesetter provides many benefits. Work can be done faster, more professionally, and at lower cost.

----

(1)William W. Maxey, Printing Technology (Atlanta: Eagle Press, 1983), p. 112.

REPORTS/TYPESET 012185

Figure 15.1 Report Page Showing Long Quotation and Diskette Notation

Therefore, a notation giving the name or number of the diskette on which the report is stored should be made on each report. The notation may appear only at the end of the last page, or it may appear at the bottom of each page. If it is placed only on the last page of the report, it is entered as though it were text. If the notation is to appear on all pages, it should be entered automatically as a bottom-line entry. In Figure 15.1, the diskette notation means the report is saved under the name *TYPESET 012185* on a diskette labeled *REPORTS*. If there is more than one diskette labeled *REPORTS*, each of them is also labeled by date. Review Lesson 9 for more details on using diskette notations.

USING *APPLE WRITER* FOR THE FINAL TOUCHES

Apple Writer has features that make the entry of long quotations and diskette notations quite simple. These features are discussed in the following sections.

Entering Long Quotations

To change the margins and line interval for a long quotation, you can use text-embedded print commands. Remember from Lesson 14 that each of these commands must be on a separate line with a RETURN before and after it. In other words, you press RETURN, enter the text-embedded print command, and press RETURN again. Figure 15.2 shows an example of how these commands may be used. Refer to it as you study the following instructions.

As you might suspect, the left margin is changed with a command of *.LM* and the right margin is changed by using *.RM* as the command. The margin setting may be given either as an absolute value or as a relative value. If you use an absolute value, specify the exact column number for the margin. If you use a relative value, specify the number of columns left or right that the margin should be moved. For example, to change the left margin from 10 to 15, you could use either *.LM15* or *.LM+5* as the command. To change the right margin from 75 to 70, you could use either *.RM70* or *.RM-5* as the command. It is easier to use the relative values (+5 and -5) since you do not have to remember where the margins were originally set. After the long quotation is finished, the margins are set back to their original values with an *.LM-5* or *.LM10* command and an *.RM+5* or *RM75* command.

To change the line interval to zero for the long quotation, use *.LI0* as the text-embedded command. After entering the long quotation, set the line interval back to one by using *.LI1* as the command.

Printing a Diskette Notation

A text-embedded command is also used to print a diskette notation at the bottom of each report page. *Apple Writer*'s bottom-

```
the codes telling the composer to use a
predetermined size, style, and format for
the introduction of a book.  According to
Maxey, this has great impact:
.LM+5
.RM-5
.LI0
       The translation of word processor
codes to those required by typesetting
equipment has the potential of producing
the greatest change ever seen in the
printing industry.  Its impact has
already been felt and will be felt to a
much greater extent than anyone would
have imagined just a few years
ago. (footnote reference)
.LM-5
.RM+5
.LI1
       Once the translation process is
complete, the finished document is
displayed on a CRT.  On the screen, all
```

Figure 15.2 Text-Embedded Commands for Long Quotation

line entry works just like its top-line entry if *.BL* is used instead of *.TL* as the command. If necessary, review the process given in Lesson 14. Since the diskette notation should appear at the left edge of the page, remember to enter the remaining delimiters. If the diskette notation is *REPORTS/TYPESET 012185*, for example, you might enter a command of *.BL*REPORTS/TYPESET 012185****.

Apple Writer does not know the bottom-line entry exists until it prints the part of the document where the command appears. Therefore, be sure to place the command before the end of the first page. A good place to put it is at the beginning of the text.

LESSON 15 EXERCISE Name ____________________ Date __________

TRUE/FALSE

Each of the following statements is either true or false. Indicate your choice in the Answers column by circling T for a true statement or F for a false statement.

		Answers		
1.	A long quotation is one that is over five lines long (Obj. 1)	1.	T	F
2.	Indenting the left margin 10 spaces will properly format a long quotation (Obj. 1)	2.	T	F
3.	If the right margin of a report has been set at 90, it is moved to 85 for a long quotation (Obj. 1)	3.	T	F
4.	Long quotations are printed with a line interval of zero (Obj. 1)..........	4.	T	F
5.	To change *Apple Writer*'s margins during printing, you should use the Print/Program Commands menu (Obj. 2)	5.	T	F
6.	Changes in the left and right margins may be given as absolute numbers or as relative numbers (Obj. 2)	6.	T	F
7.	The command *.LM* is used to change the left margin during printing (Obj. 2)	7.	T	F
8.	If the right margin is currently set at 90, the commands *.RM85* and *.RM+5* will have the same effect (Obj. 2)	8.	T	F
9.	You must press RETURN before and after entering a text-embedded print command (Obj. 2)	9.	T	F
10.	The line interval is changed during printing by using a text-embedded command (Obj. 3)	10.	T	F
11.	A line interval of one will cause the paper to move up one line at the end of each line of printing (Obj. 3)	11.	T	F
12.	A diskette notation must appear at the bottom of each page of a report (Obj. 4)	12.	T	F
13.	A diskette notation is printed on a report to make it easier to find the report on diskette (Obj. 4)	13.	T	F
14.	The *.BL* command is used to print a diskette notation on each page (Obj. 4)	14.	T	F

ERROR DETECTION

Part of a text page containing a long quotation and a diskette notation is reproduced below. Each line of format entries in the left column of text may be correct or incorrect. In the Answers column, write a *C* if the line is correct, write *delete* if the line should be removed, or rewrite the line correctly if it is incorrect. If necessary, add new format commands. (Note: The text would normally appear on the screen in regular report format. It is widely spaced here to allow for the insertion of any needed new lines.) (Objs. 2, 3, 4, 5)

Text as Entered	**Answers**
.BL **REPORTS/TYPESET 012185**	1.________________
the new instrument, according to its manufacturer, lifts standards to a new high:	
.LM+5	2.________________
.RM-5	3.________________
.LI1	4.________________
The Grape synthesizer provides the most technologically advanced sound envelope of any instrument thus far brought to market. In addition, its keyboard moves the leading edge of technology a quantum leap into the future. (Footnote reference)	5.________________
.RM+5	6.________________
.LM-5	7.________________
.LI0.	8.________________

COMPUTER EXERCISE

For this Computer Exercise, you will modify the second page of the report you entered in Lesson 14. Perform the following steps:

1. Load the report that you created in Lesson 14.
2. Insert the long quotation and diskette notation from Figure 15.1. Note that the footnote reference number has been moved from its original location in Lesson 14. Put the bottom-line entry for the diskette notation somewhere on the first page of the report so that it will be printed on both pages.
3. Save the updated text.
4. Make a backup copy of the file containing the text.
5. Load the Print/Program Value File named *REPORT FORMAT*. Enter new values for PL, TM, and BM as explained on page 104.
6. Print the report.

16. Producing a Block Style Letter

OBJECTIVES:

1. Identify the parts of a business letter.
2. Describe open punctuation.
3. Describe the procedure for producing a block style business letter with open punctuation.

The production of business letters is one of the major uses of a word processing system. After a business letter is dictated, it can be keyed into a word processing system by a secretary to produce the first draft. Some business people, however, enter first drafts themselves rather than dictating their letters to secretaries. Regardless of who enters the letter, it is saved on diskette. The author of the letter then reviews the first draft and makes any necessary changes. Only the changes have to be entered. The whole letter does not have to be redone. The new version of the letter is then saved on diskette and printed.

BLOCK STYLE LETTER

There are a number of different styles of business letters, but the block style letter is perhaps the most frequently used. It can be entered quickly because all parts of the letter begin on the left margin. There is no need to set different tabs or indentions. An example of a block style letter is illustrated in Figure 16.1.

The following paragraphs describe the procedure for entering a block style letter with *Apple Writer*. After you enter the date, press RETURN once for each line space to be left between the dateline and the letter address. Press RETURN once after each line of the letter address. Press RETURN again to enter a blank line both before and after the salutation. In the example letter in Figure 16.1, open punctuation is used. This means that no punctuation is entered after the salutation or the complimentary close.

Enter the body of a letter in the same way that you enter a report; that is, press RETURN only at the end of each paragraph.

Press RETURN after each of the lines in the complimentary close, typed name, typed title, reference initials, and diskette notation. Also, leave a blank line before and after the reference initials.

```
September 20, 19--  <------------  Dateline



Mrs. Mona W. Powell                    }
Director of Educational Media          }  <---  Letter Address
City Middle Schools                    }
Fayetteville, NC 28303-3882            }

Dear Mrs. Powell  <------------  Salutation

Thank you for your letter inquiring about our software products.
Our current line of software products includes software designed
for all grade levels and subject areas.  The software packages
should be used to help students become proficient as they learn
from their textbooks.

I am enclosing a catalog that lists the software products, their
prices, and ordering information.  Also enclosed is a sample
diskette for you to review some of our most popular software
products.  You should feel free to keep this diskette so that
teachers in your school system can review the programs also.

Our sales representative, Miss Gail Flowers, will call you soon.
She will be able to answer any questions you may have.

Sincerely  <------------  Complimentary Close



Mark J. Weinland, Manager  }  <---  Typed Name, Typed Title
Southern Regional Sales    }

rz:M317  <------------  Reference Initials and Diskette Notation

Enclosures  <------------  Enclosure Notation
```

Figure 16.1 Block Style Letter with Open Punctuation

SETTING THE PRINT FORMAT VALUES

As is the case with other documents, the format of a letter is determined by using the Print/Program Commands menu. The top margin can be controlled in one of two ways. One way is to vertically position the letterhead paper at the point where the date is to be printed. In this case, *TM* (top margin) on the Print/Program Commands menu is set to *0* (zero). Note: If *TM* is set to *0*, the first line of your letter may be indented one space. This cannot be avoided. Another way of controlling the top margin is to align the top edge of the letterhead paper with the top edge of the print head.

In this case, *TM* must be set to equal the number of blank lines required to print the date on the desired line.

The left and right margins are set as desired. Most businesses use a standard 6-inch-wide line. To use a 6-inch line, set *LM* (left margin) to *12* and *RM* (right margin) to *72* for 10 CPI (characters per inch). For 12 CPI, set *LM* to *15* and *RM* to *87*. The position of the firm's name on their letterhead paper sometimes determines what the left and right margins should be. The line interval *(LI)* should be set to *0* (zero) since business letters are usually single-spaced. The blank lines required in a letter are entered by pressing RETURN, as explained above. Print Mode *(PM)* is usually set to left justify *(LJ)* for letters, although some businesses use left and right justified margins *(FJ)*. Set *SP* (single page) to *1* (one) if single-sheet paper is used. When you set *SP* to *1* and enter *[P]* and then *NP*, you will be prompted with *[Insert Sheet, Press Return]*. Insert and align the letterhead page before pressing RETURN.

LESSON 16 EXERCISE Name ______________________ Date __________

TRUE/FALSE

Each of the following statements is either true or false. Indicate your choice in the Answers column by circling T for a true statement or F for a false statement.

		Answers		
1.	In a block style letter, the date is centered (Obj. 1)	1.	T	F
2.	The closing lines of a block style letter begin at the left margin (Obj. 1)	2.	T	F
3.	To put the desired number of line spaces between the dateline and the letter address, you should press RETURN the correct number of times (Obj. 3)	3.	T	F
4.	Open punctuation means there is no punctuation after the salutation or after the complimentary close (Obj. 2)	4.	T	F
5.	When you enter the body of a letter, you press RETURN at the end of each line (Obj. 3)	5.	T	F
6.	*TM* should be set to *0* (zero) if the letterhead paper is positioned in the printer at the point where the date is to be printed (Obj. 3)	6.	T	F
7.	To use a 6-inch-wide line when printing at 10 CPI, set *LM* to *0* and *RM* to *60* (Obj. 3)	7.	T	F
8.	*LI* should be set to *1* for single spacing when printing a letter (Obj. 3)...	8.	T	F
9.	*SP* is set to *1* when using continuous-form paper (Obj. 3)	9.	T	F
10.	*PM* is set for *RJ* when printing a letter (Obj. 3)	10.	T	F

COMPUTER EXERCISE

1. Enter the following letter in block style with open punctuation. Each (P) in the copy indicates that a new paragraph should be started at that point.

```
March 12, 19-- Mr. Charles E. Cobbins  Manager
Advertising MicroChips Manufacturing, Inc.
49825 El Camino Real  San Jose, CA 95129-9778
Dear Mr. Cobbins  Thank you for your inquiry
about our advertising services.  In addition
to being known for exciting television
commercials, we also have a print advertising
department which specializes in four-color
process, computer-generated graphics, multiple
type fonts, and writers who produce some of
the most creative copy in the business. (P) I
am inviting you to meet with members of our
staff on March 27 at 9:00 a.m.  In this
meeting you will have the opportunity to
discuss your next fall's advertising campaign.
(P) I look forward to hearing from you soon to
confirm this appointment.  Please call if I
can answer any questions.  Sincerely Lisa Y.
Cruz  Vice President, Marketing ck:M104
```

2. Use the following information for setting the print format values: Set the top margin for 2 inches, and set the side margins using a 70-space line.
3. Save the letter using the guidelines for naming a text file from Lesson 9.
4. Save the print format values in a file named *LETTER*.
5. Print the letter.
6. Write the print format values that you used on the bottom of the letter.

17. Producing a Two-Page Modified Block Style Letter

OBJECTIVES:

1. Explain how to arrange the parts of a modified block style letter.
2. Describe mixed punctuation.
3. Explain how to enter vertical and horizontal second-page headings for letters.
4. Explain how to produce a two-page, modified block style letter with mixed punctuation.

In Lesson 16 you learned how to enter a block style letter with open punctuation. In this lesson, you will learn how to enter a two-page modified block style letter with mixed punctuation.

MODIFIED BLOCK STYLE LETTER

Many people prefer the modified block style letter because of its balanced appearance. To give the letter a balanced look, the dateline, complimentary close, typed name, and typed title begin at the center point of the page. The paragraphs may be indented or not depending upon the author's preference. An example of a modified block style letter is shown in Figures 17.1a and 17.1b.

Entering a modified block style letter is similar to entering a block style letter. To determine the center starting point for the dateline, complimentary close, typed name, and typed title, you first determine the width of the line that you will use to print the letter. Usually a 6-inch line is used. To set a tab at the proper point, first clear the existing tab stops. Then divide the line length in half (30 if printing at 10 CPI or 36 if printing at 12 CPI). This is the correct number of spaces to tab from the left margin. As you strike the space bar, observe the number next to *TAB:* on the Data Line. When it displays the correct position number, set a new tab stop.

In Lesson 16 you used open punctuation. In this lesson, you will use mixed punctuation. As shown in Figure 17.1, a colon is entered after the salutation, and a comma is entered after the complimentary close.

As you did when you entered a block style letter, press RETURN for each line to be left between the dateline and the letter address. Also, press RETURN after each line of the letter address and the salutation. In the body of the letter, press RETURN only at

Dateline ⟶ September 21, 19--

Ms. Christine Keener
Manager
Marin Fashion Shoppe
845 Garden Street
San Francisco, CA 94108-2471 } ⟵ Letter Address

Dear Ms. Keener: ⟵ Salutation

Thank you for visiting with our fashion designers here in New York last week. Your ideas for next spring's designs have set off quite a wave of excitement with all of our staff.

As you requested, I am sending design sketches that include some of your suggestions. Will you review these sketches during the next two weeks? Ms. Helen Garafalo, our chief designer, plans to be on the West Coast next month and would like to review the sketches with you. She will call you soon to set up an appointment.

We are interested in promoting the "complete look." Not only do we want to manufacture and sell our designer clothes, but we would also like to offer a complete set of accessories. As you review the sketches, please consider the following:

SHOES. We would like to offer three types of shoes: casual, dress, and a shoe that can be worn on any occasion. The shoes will be manufactured from the finest leathers.

JEWELRY. Our design team suggests that the jewelry should be simple, highlighting a classically elegant look. We would like to limit our selection to earrings, necklaces, pins, and bracelets. A prime consideration is that any of the jewelry can be worn interchangeably. We plan to use both precious and semiprecious metals. The only precious stones that would be appropriate are medium- to high-quality diamonds.

HANDBAGS. We would like to offer three different handbags. A look should be created for the modern businesswoman. Perhaps a smaller handbag would be appropriate for evening and casual use. A third style designed for everyday use would complement the total selection. As with the shoes, we plan to use the best grades of leathers for manufacturing.

Figure 17.1a Modified Block Style Letter with Indented Paragraphs and Mixed Punctuation, Page 1

Ms. Christine Keener
Page 2 ← Second Page Heading
September 21, 19--

You may have other suggestions. Please feel free to discuss them with Ms. Garafalo when she visits with you.

Ms. Keener, we are very excited about working with you. Your contemporary ideas combined with our staff of innovative designers and manufacturers should prove to be most successful.

Complimentary Close → Sincerely,

Typed Name → Todd J. Beauchamps
Typed Title → Vice President, Manufacturing

ra:M244 ← Reference Initials and Diskette Notation

Enclosure ← Enclosure Notation

Figure 17.1b Modified Block Style Letter with Indented Paragraphs and Mixed Punctuation, Page 2

the end of each paragraph. The complimentary close, typed name, and typed title are entered at the same tab stop that you used to enter the dateline. The enclosure notation, reference initials, and diskette notation are entered at the left margin.

TWO-PAGE LETTER

When you are entering a letter, it is usually difficult to know if it will be longer than one page. You should first enter the letter without regard to its length. If it is longer than one page when the draft is printed, you must determine where you want the first page to end. At least two lines of the body of the letter must print on the second page.

Embedded Print Command

At the point in the text where the second page is to begin, you must enter an embedded print command. Remember that an embedded print command does not print on the document. It is used to direct the printer to perform a certain function. You must enter the embedded print command *.FF* (for form feed) in the text at the point where you want the first page to end. The printer will advance the paper to a new page. The command *.FF* must be preceded and followed by RETURN. Figure 17.2 shows part of the letter in Figure 17.1 as it would look on the monitor.

```
the shoes, we plan to use the best
grades of leathers for manufacturing.
.FF
Ms. Christine Keener
Page 2
September 21, 19--


     You may have other suggestions.
Please feel free to discuss them with
Ms. Garafalo when she visits with you.
```

Figure 17.2 Monitor Showing Use of *.FF*

Second-Page Heading

On the line after *.FF* you enter the second-page heading. There are two styles for a second-page heading. In Figure 17.1b, the vertical heading is shown. A horizontal heading may be used instead, as shown in Figure 17.3.

```
Ms. Christine Keener          Page 2          September 21, 19--
```

Figure 17.3 Horizontal Second-Page Heading

To use a horizontal heading, enter the addressee's name at the left edge of the screen (*TAB: 0* on the Data Line). Then space to the position that represents one half of the line length (30 if printing at 10 CPI; 36 if printing at 12 CPI). From this position, backspace once for every two characters or spaces in the page number. Then enter the page number. To enter the date, space to the last position for the line being used (*TAB: 60* if printing at 10 CPI; *TAB: 72* at 12 CPI). Backspace from this position once for each character or space in the date. Then enter the date.

As you can see, the vertical style is considerably easier to enter and is therefore used by more people; however, the style used is the author's preference. Regardless of the style used, two blank lines (triple spacing) should be left between the second-page heading and the remaining body of the letter. The paper should be positioned in the printer so that the second page heading will begin printing one inch (6 line spaces) from the top edge of the paper.

SETTING PRINT FORMAT VALUES

There are no special print format values to be set for either a one-page modified block style letter or a two-page letter. The top, bottom, left, and right margins are set as required. The line interval (*LI*) is usually set to *0* for single spacing, and *SP* is set to *1* if single-sheet paper is used. Remember, when *SP* is set to *1* and *[P]*, then *NP* is entered, you will be prompted with *[Insert Sheet, Press Return]*. Insert and align the letterhead page before pressing RETURN. If the letter is longer than one page, the printer will stop after the first page is printed and you will again be prompted with *[Insert Sheet, Press Return]*. At this point, remove the first sheet from the printer and insert the second sheet.

LESSON 17 EXERCISE Name ______________________ Date ____________

TRUE/FALSE

Each of the following statements is either true or false. Indicate your choice in the Answers column by circling T for a true statement or F for a false statement.

	Answers
1. In a modified block style letter, the dateline, complimentary close, typed name, and typed title begin at the left margin (Obj. 1)	1. T F
2. Paragraphs must be indented in a modified block style letter (Obj. 1)	2. T F
3. Business letters may be printed at either 10 CPI or 12 CPI (Obj. 1)	3. T F
4. To determine the starting position on the screen for the dateline of a modified block style letter, divide the line length in half (Obj. 4)	4. T F
5. *POS:* on the Data Line should be used to determine where the tab should be set for the starting position of the dateline, complimentary close, typed name, and typed title (Obj. 4)	5. T F
6. Mixed punctuation means that a comma is placed after both the salutation and the complimentary close (Obj. 2)	6. T F
7. RETURN should be pressed after each line of the letter address and salutation (Obj.4)	7. T F
8. In a modified block style letter, the enclosure notation, reference initials, and diskette notation are entered at the left margin (Obj. 1)	8. T F
9. An embedded print command prints on the document (Obj. 3)	9. T F
10. The embedded print command you enter to begin a new page is *.FF* (Obj. 3)	10. T F
11. A second-page heading of a letter includes the addressee's name and city, and the date of the letter (Obj. 3)..	11. T F
12. In the horizontal style of a second-page heading, all the information is placed on one line (Obj. 3)..	12. T F
13. To enter the date on a horizontal second-page heading, backspace once for every two characters from the center of the line (Obj. 3)	13. T F
14. If single-sheet letterhead paper is used to print a letter, the *SP* print format value is set at *0* (zero) (Obj. 4)	14. T F

COMPUTER EXERCISE

1. Enter the following letter, using the modified block style, indented paragraphs, a 70-space line, and mixed punctuation. Remember that each (P) in the copy means that a paragraph should start at that point.

March 27, 19-- Mr. LeRoy P. Boucher, President Allied Products, Inc. 3897 Poydras Avenue Baton Rouge, LA 70810-8225 Dear Mr. Boucher Thank you for your kind letter expressing your appreciation of the speech I gave in Charlotte, North Carolina. As you requested, I am outlining below the major points that I made in my presentation "How to Succeed in Your Career." (P) Specify Your Career Objectives. Your chances of achieving success are dramatically increased when you have a clear definition of your career goals. Usually this means identifying a career or profession, targeting the level you wish to achieve, and setting a definite salary level to attain. (P) Envision the Achievement of Your Goals. Many of today's professional athletes, musicians, politicians, and others dreamed of their goals on a daily basis before they became successful. Every day, you should imagine that your goal is already achieved. Whether it is catching the game-winning pass, performing at Carnegie Hall, or having your picture on the cover of <u>Time</u> magazine, you should be able to envision achieving your goal. Doing this will help supply your subconscious with an unending stream of ideas and energy that will help make these fantasies a reality. (P) Use the 80/20 Rule. Studies have shown that many people spend only 20 percent of their time on important tasks. The other 80 percent of their time is spent on matters that do not contribute to success. To make all of your efforts count, sharply define the specific results you wish to achieve. Once they are defined, then set out with zeal to accomplish them. Use 80 percent of your time to deal with those matters that will give you the greatest results. For each task, each phone call, each letter, ask yourself, "Is this bringing me closer to my goal?" (P) Stress Your Successes. Whenever you achieve excellent results or have good ideas, convey this information in a nonboastful manner. The old saying "It pays to advertise" is certainly appropriate. Always seek out those activities that will bring the greatest rewards to you. (P) Take Chances. Most people, regardless of their places in society, business, or professions, retreat from responsibility. This is perhaps where your biggest opportunity lies--the opportunity to pass them. Leaders in all facets of our society attained their status because they were willing to risk the odds. The history of our country abounds with many examples from the patriots of the Revolutionary days to today's astronauts. (P) Mr. Boucher, many people attest to this formula for success. I am sure that you can considerably increase the productivity of your employees if you share this message with them. Sincerely Mary C. Barton-Cole Management Consultant rt:C017

2. Using the following print format values, print a draft of the letter: For the side margins, use a 70-space line. Set a two-inch top margin for the first page and a one-inch top margin for the second page. Set a one-inch bottom margin.
3. Determine where the first page should end. Enter the correct embedded print command. Then enter a horizontal second-page heading.
4. Save the letter using the file name of *LESSON 17H (your name).*
5. Print a final draft of the letter.
6. Change the second-page heading to the vertical style.
7. Save the letter using the new file name of *LESSON 17V (your name).*
8. Print the letter again.
9. Write the format values you used on the bottom of each of the letters.

18. Introduction to Tables

OBJECTIVES:

1. Identify the format of a simple table.
2. Explain how to enter embedded print commands for a simple table.
3. Explain how to compute the left margin setting for a simple table.
4. Give the procedure for producing a two-column table.

One of the most useful ways to present information is in the form of a table. Information in a table is usually arranged in columns, with one or two headings. Only essential information is presented.

Word processing helps to make entering tables easy. Through the use of embedded print commands, you can direct the computer to center the heading or headings of the table. You can also use embedded print commands to set the left margin.

TABLE FORMAT

There are some rules that should be followed when entering a table. Observe the table in Figure 18.1 as you read the following explanation of table format.

```
SELECTED MANUFACTURERS OF MICROCOMPUTERS
                              DS (double space: 1 blank line)
     (Manufacturing Location)

                              TS (triple space: 2 blank lines)

Apple Computer Inc.                  California
Commodore International Ltd.         Pennsylvania
IBM Corp.                            Florida
Tandy Corp.                          Texas
Texas Instruments Inc.               Texas
```

Figure 18.1 Two-Column Table with Main and Secondary Headings

The main heading of a table is always entered in all caps. You may recall that *[K]* (alpha lock) is used to enter a row of capital letters. If there is a secondary heading such as in Figure 18.1, double space after the main heading by pressing RETURN twice. This leaves one blank line space. Secondary headings are entered with only the first letter of each major word capitalized. Leave a triple space after a main heading if there is no secondary heading. Always leave a triple space after a secondary heading. To triple-space, press RETURN three times, leaving two blank line spaces. The body of the table may be either single-spaced or double-spaced, depending upon the preference of the author. The left and right margins of the table are determined by the length of the longest line in the table.

ENTERING A TABLE

The first procedure to follow before entering a table is to turn off word wrap. To do this, enter *[Z]*. The *Z* on the Data Line is removed, indicating that word wrap is turned off. Turning off word wrap helps you in lining up columns.

The next step to follow before entering the table is to set up a series of embedded print commands. Observe Figure 18.2, which shows the table from Figure 18.1 as it would appear on the monitor with word wrap disabled. Recall that embedded print commands may be in either uppercase or lowercase letters.

```
.LIO
.LM1
.RM80
.CJ
SELECTED MANUFACTURERS OF MICROCOMPUTERS

(Manufacturing Location)


.LJ
.LM17
Apple Computer Inc.                    California
Commodore International Ltd.           Pennsylvania
IBM Corp.                              Florida
Tandy Corp.                            Texas
Texas Instruments Inc.                 Texas
```

Figure 18.2 Two-Column Table with Embedded Print Commands

You may recall from previous lessons that the purpose of an embedded print command is to direct *Apple Writer* to perform a certain function while it is printing. Embedded print commands are not printed on the document. Also, recall that each embedded print command must appear on a line by itself, and it must be preceded by a period.

The first embedded print command that you enter in the table, *.LI0*, sets the line interval to *0* (zero), for single spacing. *LI* could be set to either *1* or *2* for double or triple spacing if desired. Setting *.LM* (left margin) to *1* and *.RM* (right margin) to *80* (or *102* if printing at 12 CPI) allows the headings to be centered on the sheet of paper. The command *.CJ* (center justify) instructs *Apple Writer* to horizontally center the lines that follow until it finds *.LJ* (left justify). When the *.LJ* command is encountered, all remaining lines are left justified until another justify command is encountered.

The main heading is entered in all caps, beginning at the left edge of the screen. Double-space and then enter the secondary heading, followed by a triple space. Remember to enter *.LJ* after you have entered the headings.

The setting for the *.LM* command immediately before the body of the table is determined after all the tab stops have been set. To set the tab stops and the left margin, use the following procedures:

1. Enter *[Z]* to disable word wrap.
2. Clear all tab stops by entering *[T]* and then *P* (for purge).
3. Determine the number of spaces to leave between the columns of information.
4. With *TAB: 0* on the Data Line, space forward once for each character or space of the longest line in the first column. Then space forward the number of spaces you have decided to leave between the columns.
5. Enter *[T]* and *S* to set a tab stop at this point for the beginning of the second column.
6. Space forward once for each character or space of the longest line in the second column. If there are more than two columns in the table, continue to space forward, leaving the desired number of spaces between columns and setting the tab stops. Always space forward for the longest line in the last column.
7. Observe the *TAB:* number on the Data Line. Subtract the *TAB:* number from the *.RM* setting (*80* at 10 CPI) and divide by 2. This gives you the left margin setting.
8. Use the backspace key to return to *TAB: 0* position.
9. Enter *.LM* and the number computed in Step 7.

You are now ready to enter the body of the table. Enter each line in order as it appears. Remember to enter *[I]* to tab to each tab stop.

LESSON 18 EXERCISE Name ______________________ Date ____________

TRUE/FALSE

Each of the following statements is either true or false. Indicate your choice in the Answers column by circling T for a true statement or F for a false statement.

		Answers	
1.	The main heading of a table is entered in all caps (Obj. 1)	1. T	F
2.	Between a main heading and a secondary heading, leave a triple space (Obj. 1)	2. T	F
3.	Between a secondary heading or main heading and the body of a table, leave a double space (Obj. 1)	3. T	F
4.	To leave a double space, press RETURN twice (Obj. 1)	4. T	F
5.	The left margin of a table is determined by adding the lengths of longest lines in all columns (Obj. 3)	5. T	F
6.	Before entering a table, *[Z]* should be entered (Obj. 4)	6. T	F
7.	Embedded print commands must be entered in all caps (Obj. 2)	7. T	F
8.	*.LI1* sets single spacing (Obj. 2)	8. T	F
9.	To center table headings, *.RJ* should be entered immediately before the headings (Obj. 2)	9. T	F
10.	To clear all tab stops, enter *[T]* and then *P* (Obj. 4)	10. T	F
11.	To determine the *TAB:* number to be used in computing the left margin setting, space forward once for each character or space of the longest line in each column (Obj. 3)	11. T	F
12.	To determine the left margin setting for the body of a table, subtract the *TAB:* number from the *.RM* setting and divide by 2 (Obj. 3)	12. T	F

COMPUTER EXERCISE

1. Enter the following table. Single-space the body.

SELECTED STATES AND THEIR CAPITAL CITIES

(In Alphabetic Order)

Alabama	Montgomery
California	Sacramento
Georgia	Atlanta
Hawaii	Honolulu
New Hampshire	Concord
North Carolina	Raleigh
Pennsylvania	Harrisburg
Tennessee	Nashville
Texas	Austin

2. Save the table using the file name *lesson 18 (your name).*
3. Print the table.
4. On the bottom of your printout write the values for the following embedded print commands you used:

.LI

.LM (before the headings)

.RM

.LM (before the body of the table)

19. Entering a Multi-Column Table

OBJECTIVES:

1. Describe the procedure for entering underlined column headings.
2. Describe the procedure for entering dollar amounts and totals in the body of a table.
3. Describe the procedure for entering a source line.

In Lesson 18 you learned how to enter a two-column table with a main heading and a secondary heading. You may have more than two columns in a table. The only limit to the number of columns is the number of print positions on the paper. In addition to main and secondary headings, tables frequently have column headings that describe the types of information presented in the columns. The column headings may be underlined to highlight their appearance.

Tables are often used to present financial information such as accounting and budget reports. Financial information usually includes dollar amounts, as shown in Figure 19.1.

STATUS OF DEPARTMENTAL BUDGETS

For the Month Ending March 31, 19--

Department	Budget	Total Obligations
Accounting	$ 150,000.00	$ 10,564.23
Advertising & Promotion	175,000.00	104,269.43
Distribution	250,000.00	9,671.90
Manufacturing	500,000.00	162,870.93
Marketing	200,000.00	92,481.62
Personnel	125,000.00	68,356.91
Sales	300,000.00	118,943.02
	-------------	-----------
Total	$1,700,000.00	$567,158.04

Source: Business Plan

Figure 19.1 Three-Column Table with Column Headings

TABLE FORMAT

Refer to Figure 19.1 while reading this section. When column headings are entered, they are treated as part of the body of the table. Use a line interval of 2 between the main heading and the column headings if there is no secondary heading. If there is a secondary heading, use a line interval of 2 after the secondary heading and a line interval of 1 after the main heading. Always use a line interval of 1 after column headings regardless of the line interval used in the body of the table.

You may recall that *Apple Writer* has a feature that underlines characters. This feature underlines only letters, numbers, and special symbols. It will not underline blank spaces. Therefore, the column headings in Figure 19.1 can be entered with a reverse slash before *Department* and after *Total Obligations* as follows:

\Department   Budget   Total Obligations\

To make a reverse slash on the Apple II Plus, use CTRL, SHIFT, P; on the Apple IIe, use the reverse slash key.

When dollar amounts are presented in a table, each column is aligned at the decimal point. Observe the *Budget* and *Total Obligations* columns in Figure 19.1. A dollar sign is entered on the first line of the body and on the *Total* line. It is not necessary to put dollar signs on the other lines.

If the body of the table is to be printed with a line interval of 1, the text-embedded print command *.LI1* must be entered. If the body is to be printed with a line interval of 0, the *.LI* command is not necessary.

When totals are to be printed, there must be lines separating the column amounts from the total amounts. As mentioned earlier, the underline feature underlines letters, numbers, and special characters, but not blank spaces. In Figure 19.1 it is necessary to have a line beneath the last amount in the *Budget* column that is as long as the total amount. In this case, the underline feature cannot be used. Instead, you must enter an underline on a separate line space. To do this, strike CTRL, SHIFT, and M at the same time on the Apple II Plus. Strike these three keys once for each underline space. Use the underline key on the Apple IIe. In Figure 19.1 the combination of CTRL, SHIFT, and M is struck once for each character in the *Budget* total and once for each character in the *Total Obligations* total.

When a source line is used in a table, it is separated from the body of the table with a line interval of 0 and a 1 1/2-inch underline. If the body of the table is printed with a line interval of 1, then the new text-embedded print command *.LI0* should be entered before the separator line. To enter the separator line, CTRL, SHIFT, and M should be struck 15 times (if printing at 10 CPI) or 18 times (if printing at 12 CPI) on the Apple II Plus. Strike the underline key the same number of times on the Apple IIe. Use a line interval of 1 after the underline. The word *Source* with a colon after it is entered at the left margin of the table. Space twice after the colon and enter the source of the information.

ENTERING A TABLE

The table in Figure 19.1 would appear on the screen as it looks in Figure 19.2.

```
.LI0
.LM1
.RM80
.CJ
STATUS OF DEPARTMENTAL BUDGETS

For the Month Ending March 31, 19--
.LJ

.LM9
      \Department                     Budget          Total Obligations\

Accounting                    $  150,000.00           $ 10,564.23
Advertising & Promotion          175,000.00           104,269.43
Distribution                     250,000.00             9,671.90
Manufacturing                    500,000.00           162,870.93
Marketing                        200,000.00            92,481.62
Personnel                        125,000.00            68,356.91
Sales                            300,000.00           118,943.02
                                 -------------        -----------
Total                         $1,700,000.00          $567,158.04

---------------

Source:  Business Plan
```

Figure 19.2 Table with Embedded Print Commands

Refer to Figure 19.2 as you review the following procedures for entering a table with main, secondary, and column headings, and a source line.

1. Review Lesson 18 to get the procedure for entering embedded print commands before and after the main and secondary headings.
2. If the body of the table is to be printed with double spacing, use a line interval of 1. If the body of the table is to be printed with single spacing, a line interval command is not necessary. Remember to enter *.LJ* so that the rest of the table is not center justified.

3. Enter *[Z]* to disable word wrap.
4. Clear all tab stops by entering *[T]* and then *P* (for purge).
5. Determine the number of spaces you wish to have between columns of information.
6. With *TAB: 0* on the Data Line, space forward once for each character or space of the longest line in the first column. Space forward the number of spaces to be left between columns (Figure 19.2 uses 6 spaces). Set a tab stop at this point.
7. Space forward once for each character or space of the longest line in the second column. Space forward the number of spaces to be left between columns (Figure 19.2 uses 6 spaces). Set a tab stop at this point.
8. Space forward once for each character or space for the longest line in the third column. (The column heading is the longest line in Figure 19.2.) Observe the *TAB:* number on the Data Line.
9. Subtract the *TAB:* number (in this example, *TAB: 62*) from the *.RM* setting (*.RM80*) and divide by two (80 − 62 = 18; 18 ÷ 2 = 9). This gives you the left margin setting (*.LM9*).
10. Backspace to return to *TAB: 0* position. Enter *.LM9*. Then enter *.LI1* if the body of the table is to printed with double spacing. Otherwise the *.LI* command is not necessary.
11. To enter the column headings, follow these procedures:
    a. From *TAB: 0*, space forward once for each two characters or spaces of the longest line in Column 1 (*Advertising & Promotion*). Drop the extra letter and use only even numbers. This puts the cursor at center point of the first column.
    b. Then backspace once for each two characters or spaces in the column heading. Drop the extra letter, if any, and use only even numbers.
    c. Enter *CTRL, SHIFT*, and *P* at the same time to use the underline feature on the Apple II Plus. Enter the reverse slash on the Apple IIe. Then enter the heading *Department*.
    d. Tab to the beginning of the second column and follow Steps a and b of this section. Then enter the heading *Budget*.
    e. Tab to the beginning of the third column. Here the procedure changes because the column heading is

the longest line. Simply enter the heading *Total Obligations,* and follow it with a reverse slash.

12. If the body of the table is to be single-spaced, press RETURN twice after the line of column headings to get double spacing. Otherwise begin entering the body of the table after pressing RETURN once.
13. After you have entered the body of the table, the text-embedded command *.LI0* must be entered if the body of the table was double-spaced. If it was single-spaced, a new command is not necessary. Then enter *CTRL, SHIFT,* and *M* 15 times for a 1 1/2-inch separator line if printing at 10 CPI or 18 times if printing at 12 CPI. On the Apple IIe, use the underline key.
14. Double space after the separator line and enter the source line.

LESSON 19 EXERCISE Name ______________________ Date ____________

TRUE/FALSE

Each of the following statements is either true or false. Indicate your choice in the Answers column by circling T for a true statement or F for a false statement.

		Answers	
1.	Use a line interval of 1 between a main heading and column headings (Obj. 1)	1. T	F
2.	If there is a secondary heading, use a line interval of 2 between the secondary heading and the column headings (Obj. 1)	2. T	F
3.	Always use a line interval of 1 between column headings and the body of the table (Obj. 1)	3. T	F
4.	Dollar amounts in columns are aligned at the decimal point (Obj. 2)	4. T	F
5.	It is not necessary to enter a dollar sign before each dollar amount (Obj. 2)	5. T	F
6.	If the body of a table is to be entered with a line interval of 0, the *.LI* command is not necessary (Obj. 2)	6. T	F
7.	The line beneath the last amount in a column should be as long as the number of characters in the amount above it (Obj. 2)	7. T	F
8.	Use of the underline causes letters, numbers, and spaces to be underlined (Obj. 2)	8. T	F
9.	A blank line space must be entered before entering the line above the total (Obj. 2)	9. T	F
10.	A source line is separated from the body of the table with a line interval of 1 (Obj. 3)	10. T	F
11.	When printing at 10 CPI, the source line length is 15 underscores (Obj. 3)	11. T	F
12.	The word *Source* is entered at the left margin with a double space after the colon (Obj. 3)	12. T	F

COMPUTER EXERCISE

1. Enter the following table. The body of the table should have a line interval of 1. Leave 6 spaces between columns.

TYPICAL MONTHLY FAMILY BUDGET

(By Family Size)

Category	Two	Four
Rent or Mortgage	$ 600.00	$ 900.00
Food	100.00	200.00
Clothing	150.00	250.00
Utilities	40.00	75.00
Transportation	125.00	200.00
Personal Expenses	200.00	350.00
Education/Entertainment	125.00	300.00
Savings	100.00	125.00
Totals	$1,440.00	$2,400.00

Source: Estimates

2. Save the table.
3. Load the Print/Program Value File.
4. Print the table.

NAME ______________________ DATE __________

20. Theory Test 2

In this lesson you will test your knowledge of the concepts and procedures you have learned in Lessons 12 through 19.

TRUE/FALSE

Each of the following statements is either true or false. Indicate your choice in the Answers column by circling T for a true statement or F for a false statement. NOTE: The objective number in parentheses following each question refers to the lesson number and corresponding objective number. For example, Obj. 12-1 indicates that the question was discussed in Lesson 12 and refers to the first objective in that lesson.

	Answers
1. Computers used for word processing are very reliable. Therefore, duplicate copies of important files are not needed (Obj. 12-1)	1. **T F**
2. Initializing a diskette erases everything that may have been saved on the diskette (Obj. 12-2)	2. **T F**
3. When a file is being saved onto a backup diskette, the original and backup diskettes must both be in disk drives at the same time (Obj. 12-3)	3. **T F**
4. Saving a backup file can be done with one disk drive. However, to duplicate an entire diskette, two disk drives are necessary (Obj. 12-3)	4. **T F**
5. The option to duplicate an entire diskette is selected from *Apple Writer*'s DOS Commands menu (Obj. 12-4)	5. **T F**
6. To save a backup copy of a file, you must use a program on the Apple system master diskette (Obj. 12-4)	6. **T F**
7. The space between the edge of the paper and the printed words is known as a margin (Obj. 13-2)	7. **T F**
8. The top margin on the first page of a report is usually 1 inch (Obj. 13-2)	8. **T F**
9. The right and left margins of an unbound report are the same size (Obj. 13-2)	9. **T F**
10. Right justification causes all lines to begin at the left margin and end evenly at the right margin (Obj. 13-3)	10. **T F**
11. Print format can be controlled from the Print/Program Commands menu (Obj. 13-3)	11. **T F**
12. Text-embedded print commands become effective when they are found by *Apple Writer* as it prints text (Obj. 13-3)	12. **T F**
13. By using reverse slashes, you can cause *Apple Writer* to underline words (Obj. 13-3)	13. **T F**

14. The top margin on the second page of a report is 1 inch (Obj. 14-1) ...... 14. **T** **F**
15. The top-line entry on a report may contain information other than the page number (Obj. 14-2)...... 15. **T** **F**
16. *Apple Writer*'s top-line entry feature allows the printing of up to three different items at the top of each page (Obj. 14-3) ...... 16. **T** **F**
17. *Apple Writer* automatically places footnotes at the bottom of the page on which they are entered (Obj. 14-3) ...... 17. **T** **F**
18. When using *Apple Writer*, you should enter a footnote immediately following its reference in the text (Obj. 14-3) ...... 18. **T** **F**
19. Either the Print/Program Commands menu or text-embedded commands may be used for printing a top-line entry (Obj. 14-3) ...... 19. **T** **F**
20. Indenting the left margin 10 spaces will properly format a long quotation (Obj. 15-1) ...... 20. **T** **F**
21. If the right margin of a report has been set at 90, it is moved to 85 for a long quotation (Obj. 15-1) ...... 21. **T** **F**
22. Changes in the left and right margins may be given as absolute numbers or as relative numbers (Obj. 15-2)...... 22. **T** **F**
23. The command *.LJ* is used to change the left margin during printing (Obj. 15-2) ...... 23. **T** **F**
24. If the right margin is currently set at 90, the commands *.RM85* and *.RM+5* will have the same effect (Obj. 15-2)...... 24. **T** **F**
25. You must press RETURN before and after entering a text-embedded print command (Obj. 15-2)...... 25. **T** **F**
26. The *.BL* command can be used to print a diskette notation on each page (Obj. 15-4) ...... 26. **T** **F**
27. The closing lines of a block style letter begin at the left margin (Obj. 16-1) 27. **T** **F**
28. Open punctuation means there is no punctuation after the salutation or after the complimentary close (Obj. 16-2) ...... 28. **T** **F**
29. *TM* should be set to 0 if the letterhead paper is positioned in the printer at the point where the date is to be printed (Obj. 16-3) ...... 29. **T** **F**
30. *LI* should be set to 1 for single spacing when printing a letter (Obj. 16-3) 30. **T** **F**
31. *SP* is set to 1 when using continuous-form paper (Obj. 16-3) ...... 31. **T** **F**
32. *PM* should be set for *RJ* when printing a letter (Obj. 16-3) ...... 32. **T** **F**
33. In a modified block style letter, the dateline, complimentary close, typed name, and typed title begin at the left margin (Obj. 17-1) ...... 33. **T** **F**
34. Business letters may be printed at either 10 CPI or 12 CPI (Obj. 17-1) ... 34. **T** **F**
35. To determine the starting position on the screen for the dateline of a modified block style letter, divide the line length in half (Obj. 17-1) ...... 35. **T** **F**
36. *POS:* on the Data Line should be used to determine where the tab should be set for the starting position of the dateline, complimentary close, typed name, and typed title (Obj. 17-4) ...... 36. **T** **F**

37. In the horizontal style of a second-page heading, all the information is placed on one line (Obj. 17-3) .... 37. **T** **F**

38. If single-sheet letterhead paper is used to print a letter, the *SP* print format value is set to 0 (Obj. 17-4) .... 38. **T** **F**

39. Between a secondary heading or main heading and the body of a table, leave a double space (Obj. 18-1) .... 39. **T** **F**

40. The left margin of a table is determined by the longest line in each column (Obj. 18-3) .... 40. **T** **F**

41. Before entering a table, *[Z]* should be entered (Obj. 18-2) .... 41. **T** **F**

42. To center table headings, *.RJ* should be entered immediately before the headings (Obj. 18-2) .... 42. **T** **F**

43. To determine the *TAB:* number in computing the left margin setting, space forward once for each character or space of the longest line in each column (Obj. 18-3) .... 43. **T** **F**

44. To determine the left margin setting for the body of a table, subtract the *TAB:* number from the *.RM* setting and divide by 2 (Obj. 18-3) .... 44. **T** **F**

45. If a table has a secondary heading, you should use a line interval of 2 between the secondary heading and the column headings (Obj. 19-1) .... 45. **T** **F**

46. When entering a table, dollar amounts in columns are entered aligned at the decimal point (Obj. 19-2) .... 46. **T** **F**

47. When entering dollar amounts in a table, it is not necessary to enter the dollar sign before each amount (Obj. 19-2) .... 47. **T** **F**

48. If the body of a table is to be entered with a line interval of 0, the *.LI* command is not necessary (Obj. 19-2) .... 48. **T** **F**

49. If the total line is longer than the number that precedes it, a separate line space must be used before entering the total line (Obj. 19-2) .... 49. **T** **F**

50. A source line is separated from the body of the table with a line interval of 1 (Obj. 19-3) .... 50. **T** **F**

21. Skill Test 2

In this lesson you will produce a letter and a report from unarranged copy. Be sure to correct your errors.

1. Enter the following letter in block style with open punctuation. Use a 60-space line. Save it with the file name *LESSON 21 LETTER (your name).*

```
May 1, 19-- Dr. Alice Vale  389 Regal Way
Rochester, NY 14621-1239  Dear Dr. Vale
As you requested, we have completed a survey
of available medical office property in
metropolitan Rochester.  The enclosed report
will give you the full details of our
findings.  (P) As you would suspect, the
properties closer to the better hospitals tend
to have more space and carry higher asking
prices.  Those in more remote locations tend
to be smaller and less expensive.  (P) As
was discussed earlier, we are ready to enter
negotiations for you on any property.  We also
look forward to managing the units for you
once a building has been purchased.  Sincerely
Brannon Randall Broker  ct:C21  Enclosure
```

2. Enter the following report in correct format. The table appearing in the report should be single-spaced and properly centered. The footnote should be entered so that it appears at the bottom of the page when the report is printed. Use a bottom-line entry to place a diskette notation of *REPORTS/VALE 0501--* at the bottom of each page. Save the report with the file name *LESSON 21 REPORT (your name).*

SURVEY OF AVAILABLE MEDICAL OFFICE PROPERTY
COMPILED FOR DR. ALICE VALE
MAY 1, 19--
(P) As of this date, five medical office complexes are on the market. They range in size from two suites to twelve. Here are the available units, ranked from most expensive to least expensive:

Location	Hospital	Suites	Asking Price
Forest Court	Willowbrook	12	3,400,000
40 Arrowood Drive	Willowbrook	5	990,000
1243 Peach	Southside	4	720,000
96 Rock Springs	Wyley General	3	360,000
132 Beech Street	Wyley General	2	93,000

(P) The Forest Court property is contemporary in architectural style and features soaring atriums and plenty of glass. One of the first medical buildings to make use of solar heating, it is really spectacular. The tenants here are nationally known specialists in their areas. The complex is contiguous to Willowbrook Medical Center, with a skywalk connecting the two complexes. Arrowood is approximately one mile from Willowbrook and features Williamsburg-style architecture. It is somewhat older than Forest Court. (P) The only complex available near Southside Hospital is the Peach facility. It is of contemporary design with stone facades as its outstanding architectural feature. It is four blocks from Southside. (P) Two facilities are available near the almost rural Wyley General Hospital. The complex on Rock Springs features Williamsburg-style architecture and is four years old. It is one mile from the hospital but has very convenient access with no stop signs, no traffic signals and almost no traffic between there and the hospital. The Beech facility, containing only two small suites, can best be described architecturally as "commercial steel," having very little character of any kind. It is only one mile from the hospital, but access is hindered by the circuitous nature of the streets and a railroad crossing with no underpass or overpass. (P) All the properties are presently in good condition and fully rented except for Forest Court, which has one vacancy. This is the first vacancy in the complex since it was completed six years ago. Negotiations are now under way between the present owner and a prospective tenant. (P) Present rental rates in all units appear to be satisfactory for your objectives, though the Beech location is marginally so. We are now in the process of preparing a detailed financial comparison for you. (P) The Arrowood location is the object of a suit (Footnote this as: Suit by a contractor, Global Electronic Security, Inc., against the current owner of the building, KFX Properties, Ltd.) that is on the calendar for trial shortly. Our opinion is that this suit will be settled in a way not derogatory to your welfare if you should decide on that property. However, we would suggest awaiting its outcome (since that should be no more than a few weeks) before entering into a contract. (P) Full details

```
on the facilities at each location are
included in the attachments to this summary
report.  Any other desired information will
be obtained as quickly as possible for you.
```

3. Print the letter and the report.

22. Merging Documents

OBJECTIVES:

1. Describe the process of merging documents.
2. Describe three applications of merging documents.
3. Give the procedure for merging *Apple Writer* files.

One of the valuable features of a word processor is its ability to merge two or more documents. Merging of documents is useful in many applications.

DEFINITION OF MERGING

Merging is the process of putting together one or more text files to create a new document. First, one text file is loaded into the computer's memory. Then, without erasing the first document, a second file is loaded. Since the loading of a file for merging does not erase the text already in memory, the contents of the files become merged; that is, they are put together.

If you wish to save the merged text, the usual save command may be used. If the merged text is considered to be temporary, you may print it without saving it to diskette.

APPLICATIONS OF MERGED FILES

There are many uses for merged files. Some of them are described in the following examples.

Merging a Table into a Report

Suppose a table giving the names of typesetting consultants has been prepared. At a later time the table is needed as part of a report. The table can simply be merged from its current diskette file into the report rather than reentered.

Merging a Table into a Letter

A school may keep a list of all its extracurricular activities and faculty sponsors. Later the school sends a letter to students inviting them to become involved in activities. The list of activities and sponsors can be merged into the letter of invitation.

Merging the Same Information into Several Documents

In the sale of a house a legal description of the house and its land may be required in several different legal documents. This description, which includes the exact location and size of the property, may be rather lengthy. If it is entered once and saved to diskette, it can then be merged into all the required legal forms without rekeying.

USING *APPLE WRITER* TO MERGE DOCUMENTS

Apple Writer's load command is used to merge one document into another. This is possible because the load command does not erase the contents of the computer's memory when it reads a file off the diskette.

The first step in merging is to have some text in the computer's memory. This text may be loaded from diskette or it may be entered from the keyboard. There must be an additional text file on diskette; this additional file will be merged with the text already in memory. If text from one document is to be placed in the middle of the other document, the "surrounding" document must be in memory first. Then the second document is loaded into its proper position.

As an example, suppose you have a list of dealers' names and addresses stored on diskette under the name *DEALERS INDIANA SOUTH BEND.* The contents of this file might be similar to the one shown in Figure 22.1. In response to a customer's inquiry, you want to send a letter containing the names and addresses of the dealers. Refer again to Figure 22.1 to see such a letter as it might be entered from the keyboard. Once the letter is in the computer's memory, the file of dealers' names and addresses may be merged with it. If desired, additional text may be keyed in after the merge.

Here are the steps for merging documents with *Apple Writer*, using Figure 22.1 as an example:

1. Enter the letter as you normally enter any new text.
2. Move the cursor to the point at which you want the names and addresses from the diskette to be inserted.
3. Use the *[L]* command to load the file named *DEALERS INDIANA SOUTH BEND* into memory. The text from the file is inserted into the letter at the point where the cursor is positioned.
4. Save the merged document on diskette. Then a copy can be printed for mailing to Mr. Csinisek.

Letter in computer's memory:

April 21, 19--

Mr. Samuel Csinisek
9873 Eighth Avenue
South Bend, IN 46683-3729

Dear Mr. Csinisek

We are sorry you have had problems with the Wyatt Model 8 you purchased in Florida.

Normally any repair work under warranty must be performed by the selling dealer. However, since you have moved, we are authorizing the work to be done by a dealer in South Bend. Just take the unit, along with this letter, to any of the following dealers:

If you should have any further difficulty, please let us know.

Sincerely

WYATT INDUSTRIES, LTD.

Miss Helen R. Franks, Manager
Warranty Claims Department

sr:W18

File on diskette may be merged (combined) with letter in memory:

SAMPSON SPECIALTIES
32 Browns Mill Road
South Bend, IN 46683-3663

JONES & ASSOCIATES
RFD 3, Box 192
South Bend, IN 46683-0192

R/M ENTERPRISES
2987 Freedom Court
South Bend, IN 46683-4829

Figure 22.1 Illustration of Merging Operation

LESSON 22 EXERCISE

Name ______________________________ Date ______________

TRUE/FALSE

Each of the following statements is either true or false. Indicate your choice in the Answers column by circling T for a true statement or F for a false statement.

	Answers		
1. Only one file at a time may be loaded into the computer's memory (Obj. 1)	1.	T	F
2. Merging allows the creation of a new document from two or more existing documents (Obj. 1)	2.	T	F
3. Merged text may be printed after its creation, but it may not be saved on diskette (Obj. 1)	3.	T	F
4. To merge two documents, they must both be saved on diskette (Obj. 1)	4.	T	F
5. There are few practical applications for merging two or more documents (Obj. 2)	5.	T	F
6. *Apple Writer* provides a special command for merging one document with another (Obj. 3)	6.	T	F
7. At least one of the two documents to be merged by *Apple Writer* must be stored on diskette (Obj. 3)	7.	T	F
8. Before merging a document from diskette into the one in memory, the cursor should be positioned at the end of the document (Obj. 3)	8.	T	F
9. A document from diskette may be placed at any desired point in the document in the computer's memory (Obj. 3)	9.	T	F
10. Once a document has been created by merging, no additional text may be entered from the keyboard (Obj. 3)	10.	T	F

MATCHING

Assume that the three files listed in Column A are included on a diskette. Each of them is to be merged with a file from Column B (also contained on diskette) to create a new document. In the first Answers column, write the letter of the file from Column A that would create a useful document when merged with the file from Column B. In the second Answers column, write the number or letter of the file that should be loaded first in order to perform the merge. (Obj. 2)

Column A	Column B	Answers
A. *DOCUMENT FOR SALE OF HOME*	1. *EXTRACURRICULAR ACTIVITIES LETTER*	1. ____ ____
B. *FACULTY SPONSORS*	2. *TABLE OF TYPESETTING CODES*	2. ____ ____
C. *TYPESETTING REPORT*	3. *LEGAL DESCRIPTION OF PROPERTY*	3. ____ ____

COMPUTER EXERCISE

In this Computer Exercise, you will create and save a table. Then you will merge the table into an already-existing report. Follow the steps below:

1. Enter the following table and save it on diskette. Use the name *CONSULTANTS* to save the file.

Myrtice Abrams	939-1194
Bryant Randleman	784-9245
Charles Tibbs	339-2389
Howard Robb	292-0367

2. Erase the computer's memory with the *[N]* command. Then load the typesetting report that you finished in Lesson 15.
3. On the second page of the report, delete the paragraph that begins "*Once the translation . . .*". Be sure to keep the footnote that precedes the paragraph.
4. At the point where you deleted the paragraph in Step 3, insert the following short paragraph. Remember to press RETURN at the end of the paragraph.

```
    Feel free to call one of the following
consultants for more information.  They are
all experts.
```

5. Make sure the cursor is still positioned on the line following the new paragraph. Then use the *[L]* command to load the file named *CONSULTANTS.*
6. Save the merged report on diskette.
7. Before printing, remember to load the Print/Program Value File named *REPORT FORMAT* and make any necessary changes in the values. Then print a copy of the report.

23. Finding and Replacing Text

OBJECTIVES:

1. Define the finding and replacing of text.
2. Describe the procedure for finding and replacing text using *Apple Writer.*
3. Use *Apple Writer* to produce form letters with customized names and addresses by using the find and replace function.

In previous lessons you learned about many of the powerful functions of a word processor. None of them, however, contribute more to the usefulness of the system than the find and replace function.

DEFINITION OF FINDING AND REPLACING

Finding and replacing is really two operations. First, a particular word, phrase, or sentence is located in the text. Then it is replaced with a new word, phrase, or sentence. If desired, the process can be repeated for all occurrences of the same part of text. This makes many editing jobs much easier. Replacement of text may be automatic, in which all occurrences of the original text are changed. Alternately, the replacement may be selective, in which the operator decides whether to change the text at each possible point of replacement.

As an example, suppose an author has just completed a novel featuring a character named Esmerelda. After completing the work, the author decides that the character should be renamed Lisa Sue. By using a simple command, all occurrences of Esmerelda in the text can be changed to Lisa Sue.

Likewise, replacement capability is useful to professionals such as attorneys. Many routine forms that must be completed are easier to do by saving the basic text, then using the find and replace function to put in the names, addresses, and so forth, of the individuals involved.

In the sales business, personalized sales letters may be produced easily. The letter is entered and saved, then individual names, addresses, and other information are entered by using the find and replace function.

If desired, the find function can be used without the replace function. This makes it easy to move the cursor to a particular point in the text, for example, or to move rapidly through the text a paragraph at a time.

USING FIND AND REPLACE WITH *APPLE WRITER*

There are quite a few variations to the find and replace function of *Apple Writer*. These variations, which add to the capability of the function, will be discussed after the basic function.

Basic Find and Replace

The find and replace function is chosen by entering *[F]*, which stands for find. The next step is to enter the text to be found and the text with which to replace it. A simple command at the end of the text may be used to specify automatic replacement. Otherwise the operator will be prompted each time the text is found. The following paragraphs describe the procedures for using the *Apple Writer* find and replace function.

When a find command is given, the search proceeds in the direction pointed by the direction arrow. (Remember that the arrow is on the Data Line at the top of the screen.) If necessary, use *[D]* to change the direction of the arrow. Do this before entering the find command. If you want the entire document to be searched, use *[B]* or *[E]* to be sure the cursor is at either the beginning or end of the text before entering the find command.

Suppose you want to change the spelling of Smythe to Smith everywhere it occurs in your text. Make sure the direction arrow is pointing to the right and the cursor is at the beginning of the text. (This would work just as well with the direction arrow pointing to the left and the cursor at the end of the text.) Then enter *[F]* to start the find and replace operation. The prompt *[F]IND:* appears at the bottom of the screen. Enter the required information so that the line appears as follows: *[F]IND:/Smythe/Smith/A*. The slashes are known as delimiters; that is, they show where the different parts of text begin and end. Note that the text to be found comes first, followed by the text to be used as a replacement. The *A* at the end (which stands for automatic and may be entered in either uppercase or lowercase) tells *Apple Writer* to replace the text everywhere it occurs without prompting the operator.

If the *A* at the end of the line is left off, the operator is requested to confirm each change before it is made. The request appears at the bottom of the screen in the following form: *[F]IND:RETURN=Proceed / Y=Replace*. By striking the Y key, the operator tells *Apple Writer* to make the replacement. If RETURN is pressed, *Apple Writer* does not make the replacement, but finds the next occurrence of the text. The find and replace function is cancelled once any other key is struck. If you want to restart a search that has been cancelled, you may enter *[F]* followed by the equals sign (=) in response to the prompt.

Find Without Replace

If you just want to find text without replacing it, you may do so with *Apple Writer*. This is an easy way to get to a particular place in the text without going through everything before it. Just enter the *[F]* command as discussed in the previous section, but do not enter replacement text. For example, to find the heading *Section III*, you enter *[F]ind:/Section III/*. The cursor stops at the desired text.

Special Delimiters

By now you may have wondered what to do if you want to find the words *January/February* and replace them with *March/April*. Since in this example a slash is part of the desired text, you cannot use the slash as the delimiter. To get around such difficulties, *Apple Writer* provides some special delimiters such as the number sign (#). You should use these special delimiters only when necessary. Always use the slash whenever possible. See Figure 23.1 for a list of the special delimiters.

Wild Cards

A wild card is a variation of find and replace which may be used to find text about which you are a little uncertain. For example, suppose that you know a document refers to several phone numbers and you want to check the numbers for accuracy. Since you entered all the numbers in the same format, you could use the following command: *[F]ind:<???-???-????<*. This command directs *Apple Writer* to find any three characters followed by a hyphen, followed by any three more characters, followed by another hyphen, followed by any four more characters. Note that the standard slash delimiter cannot be used with wild cards. The less than (<) symbol was chosen instead. (Several others are possible; see Figure 23.1.)

The preceding example of a wild card assumed text of a fixed length. Sometimes the exact length of the wild card is unknown. In such a case, use an equals sign (=) instead of the question marks. For example, suppose you can remember that a document refers to the day of the week on which an event will be held, but you do not remember which day it is. Since all days of the week end with *day*, you could use the following command: *[F]ind:< =day<*. The space in front of the equals sign indicates that there will be at least one space before the variable length of the characters in front of *day*. This variation of find and replace also works if the text you tell the computer to find is not a complete word. For example, you could search for all words that end with *ment* or *ly*. The characters used to designate fixed-length and variable-length wild cards vary depending on the delimiter chosen. See Figure 23.1 for the full list of characters.

Finding RETURN Characters

Sometimes you may want to find the places where you pressed RETURN. For example, you might want to search for RETURN characters as a quick way of scanning through text a paragraph at a time. *Apple Writer* provides several substitute characters that may be entered to search for a RETURN. This is necessary because if you really press RETURN, *Apple Writer* assumes you are finished entering the text. The character you should enter in place of RETURN depends on the delimiter you are using. For example, if you are using the number sign as the delimiter, you search for a RETURN by entering: *[F]ind:#%#*.

	CHARACTER TO USE		
Delimiter	Any-Length Wild Card	Fixed-Length Wild Card	RETURN Symbol
/	None	None	None
<	=	?	>
#	$	&	%
&	'	)	(
!	"	$	#
*	+	-	,

Figure 23.1 Possible Delimiters and Their Special Symbols

LESSON 23 EXERCISE Name ______________________ Date ____________

TRUE/FALSE

Each of the following statements is either true or false. Indicate your choice in the Answers column by circling T for a true statement or F for a false statement.

		Answers
1.	The find and replace feature of a word processor allows words or phrases to be changed to other words or phrases (Obj. 1)	1. **T** **F**
2.	The finding and replacing of text may be done only if the operator manually controls the computer keys during the find and replace process (Obj. 1)	2. **T** **F**
3.	If automatic replacement is selected, all occurrences of the specified text will be found, and replacement will take place after verification of each occurrence by the operator (Obj. 1)	3. **T** **F**
4.	In selective replacement, the operator is given the opportunity to approve or cancel each proposed change (Obj. 1)	4. **T** **F**
5.	Automatic find and replace could be appropriately used to correct the spelling of a word that had been consistently misspelled (Obj. 1)	5. **T** **F**
6.	The making of legal forms is greatly simplified by using the find and replace feature of a word processor (Obj. 1)	6. **T** **F**
7.	The find function cannot be used apart from the replace function (Obj. 2)	7. **T** **F**
8.	With *Apple Writer*, text is found and replaced by entering *[R]*, which stands for replace (Obj. 2)	8. **T** **F**
9.	The find function can find only whole words; it cannot be used to locate all occurrences of *ment*, for example (Obj. 2)	9. **T** **F**
10.	The text that is to be found and the text to which it should be changed are separated by delimiter characters (Obj. 2)	10. **T** **F**
11.	The slash mark (/) is always used with *Apple Writer* to separate the text to be found and the text to use as a replacement (Obj. 2)	11. **T** **F**
12.	The word *all* is placed at the end of the find and replace command to tell *Apple Writer* to replace all occurrences automatically (Obj. 2)	12. **T** **F**
13.	A wild card may be used to find text for which you may not know all the characters (Obj. 2)	13. **T** **F**
14.	By searching for RETURN characters, you can easily skip over entire paragraphs of text (Obj. 2)	14. **T** **F**

FIND AND REPLACE COMMANDS

For each of the following problems, write on the line the command that should be given to *Apple Writer*. (Obj. 2)

1. Find all occurrences of the word *Kathie* and automatically replace them with *Kathy*.

   [F]IND: ______________________________

2. Change occurrences of *1983* to *1984*, but only after operator confirmation.

   [F]IND: ____________________

3. Skip over a paragraph by finding the next RETURN character. Use the ampersand (&) as the delimiter.

   [F]IND: ____________________

4. Find the first occurrence of *Section II*, but do not change it.

   [F]IND: ____________________

5. A computer software company has several products whose names begin with the prefix *ULTI-*. In a document describing these products the operator mistakenly capitalized only the first letter of the prefix. Change all occurrences of *Ulti-* to *ULTI-*, regardless of the word of which it is a part. Use the number sign (#) as the delimiter.

   [F]IND: ____________________

6. Find all occurrences of stock numbers that consist of two digits, a hyphen, and four more digits. For example, *34-9782* might be one such number. Use the exclamation point as the delimiter.

   [F]IND: ____________________

COMPUTER EXERCISE

In this Computer Exercise, you will enter a form letter. Then you will customize it by inserting individual names, addresses, and other information.

1. Enter the form letter on page 172. Enter the words preceded and followed by ampersands (&) exactly as you see them. As soon as you finish entering the letter, save it on diskette.
2. Print a form letter to be sent to each of the persons listed below. Use the find and replace function to change the words preceded and followed by ampersands to the information below. Change *&sal&* to an appropriate salutation. Change the information for each customer and print the letter. Then proceed to the next customer. (Note: Be sure you enter the ampersands as part of the text to be found.)

```
Bryan L. Mann, 3987 Cypress Street, Muskegon,
MI 49440-1321
power drill

Rebecca C. Bryson, P.O. Box 39873, Richmond, VA
23224-0201
chain saw

Chad Mason, 932 Flat Creek Club Drive,
Evansville, IN 47711-2932
chain saw
```

&date&

&name&
&addr1&
&addr2&

Dear &sal&

One of the most important parts of our continuing product development process is the information received from our customers. Won't you take a moment to complete the items below? By giving us your opinion of the &product& you purchased from us, you will help us to provide better service for our customers.

_____The product suits my needs perfectly.

_____The product is satisfactory but would be better if:

_____The product has let me down in the following manner:

Thank you, &sal&, for your help. Whenever we can be of service, please let us know.

Sincerely

Pamela Russell, Manager
Product Development

24. Assembling a Document

OBJECTIVES:

1. Define document assembly.
2. Describe the process for assembling a document.
3. Assemble a document using *Apple Writer*.

There are many situations in which a business must send letters or prepare documents. Many of these documents have similar parts. In such cases, the assembly of documents by computer can save time and effort.

DEFINITION AND PURPOSE OF DOCUMENT ASSEMBLY

Assembling a document is the process of merging various presaved paragraphs into a finished document. The purpose of document assembly can best be shown by the examples in the following paragraphs.

A real estate company manages a number of apartment buildings which have several different kinds of leases. Pets are allowed in some buildings, but not in others. For those buildings in which pets are allowed, tenants who have a pet agree to pay a security deposit for the pet. Some of the buildings include the payment of utilities in the cost of the rent; others do not. By presaving paragraphs dealing with each of these variations, you can merge the appropriate paragraphs into each apartment lease as it is prepared.

When a student is suspended from school, the principal must write a letter to the student's parents. The letter must cite precisely the Board of Education rule violated by the student. For some suspensions, the student may not be on campus for any reason, such as attendance at football games. For other suspensions, attendance at school functions is allowed. The appropriate paragraphs for each situation can be loaded from the diskette and merged to make a finished letter.

An attorney prepares wills for many clients. To do so, selections are made from a large number of stock paragraphs. The chosen paragraphs are merged into finished documents that are tailored to the exact wishes of the clients.

THE ASSEMBLY PROCESS

The assembly of documents is simply a merging process. Remember from Lesson 22 that several documents may be loaded so that they are in the computer's memory at the same time, thus forming a new, larger document. To assemble a document, the merging process is simply repeated several times. Consider again the school suspension example from the previous section. Suppose that all suspensions are for either one, three, or five days. Therefore, you might have three different opening paragraphs for a suspension letter, based on the number of days of suspension. If there are 20 school board rules that can be violated, you might have 20 different paragraphs quoting and explaining these rules. You also need a paragraph to be used when the student may attend school functions and one for use when school functions may not be attended. Each of these paragraphs is entered with *Apple Writer* and saved separately. The files on diskette might be the following:

ONE DAY
THREE DAY
FIVE DAY
RULE 1
RULE 2 through *RULE 20*
ACTIVITIES
NO ACTIVITIES

If a student is to be suspended for three days for violating Rule 8 and may not attend school activities, you load the following files one after another:

THREE DAY
RULE 8
NO ACTIVITIES

As you load each file, remember to make sure the cursor is at the position where you want the paragraph added. For example, after loading the first paragraph, make sure the cursor is at the end of the text and that you press RETURN before loading the second paragraph.

Once the required paragraphs are assembled, any desired customization may be done. For example, you need to enter the parents' names and their address on the suspension letter, as well as the student's name. You might also have an individually written paragraph to add. When the letter is complete in the computer's memory, you save it to diskette and print it.

Figure 24.1 shows a completed letter that might be used by a computer software firm in responding to a request for information. Note the parts that are assembled from files on the disk and those that are entered on the keyboard.

May 22, 19--

Mrs. M. H. Lane
8 Riverwood Court
Boulder, CO 80303-3707

Dear Mrs. Lane

Entered from the keyboard.

Thanks for inquiring about our real estate property management software. Our Real Estate Management package is ideally suited for your requirements. Giving you total analysis capability as well as routine billing and accounting, this package enjoys a reputation as the best in the business.

From disk. Disk contains paragraph for each product line.

To use the programs on your SCW computer system, you will need a minimum of 128K memory and two double-density, double-sided floppy disk drives. Any 80-column printer can be used. A graphics printer, however, allows the programs to produce much nicer looking reports.

From disk. Disk contains paragraph for each popular computer.

Once you see these programs in operation, we feel sure you will agree they give exceptional performance for a very modest price. Just see one of the following dealers in your area for a demonstration:

Jones/Wright Business Systems
2987 Hill Avenue
Boulder, CO 80301-3112

Professional Software
100 Sycamore Street
Denver, CO 80301-6714

From disk. Disk contains names of dealers by geographic area.

Again, thanks for your interest. We look forward to adding your name to our list of satisfied users.

Sincerely

Jonathan Vanderslice
Marketing Manager

Standard closing lines from disk.

Figure 24.1 Assembled Letter

LESSON 24 EXERCISE Name ______________________ Date ____________

TRUE/FALSE

Each of the following statements is either true or false. Indicate your choice in the Answers column by circling T for a true statement or F for a false statement.

Answers

1. When a document is assembled, the user merges various standard paragraphs from memory (Obj. 1) .... 1. **T** **F**
2. Document assembly makes it possible to produce personalized documents from standard parts (Obj. 1) .... 2. **T** **F**
3. Since a will must be written especially for each individual, assembly with a word processor is not possible (Obj. 1) .... 3. **T** **F**
4. Different parts of text may be loaded from the disk and combined in memory to create a new document (Obj. 2) .... 4. **T** **F**
5. When a document is assembled from files on the disk, no text may be entered from the keyboard (Obj. 2) .... 5. **T** **F**
6. In assembling a document, no changes may be made in text loaded from the disk (Obj. 2) .... 6. **T** **F**
7. The assembly of documents is a merging process (Obj. 2) .... 7. **T** **F**
8. Once a document is assembled in memory, it may be saved to disk and printed (Obj. 2) .... 8. **T** **F**

COMPLETION

Assume that you are employed to prepare apartment rental leases for a large apartment management company. Your duty is to produce leases that are suited to the requirements of each apartment building and tenant. You do this by assembling each lease from previously saved parts. These parts can then be modified as necessary. The lease parts are given at the end of this section. As was done in Lesson 23, variable items in each part are indicated by a word between ampersands (&). The beginning and ending parts should be included in all leases. Other parts should be chosen when appropriate. For each of the following situations, write on the answer lines the file names of the parts that should be included in the lease. Be sure you write them in order from first to last as they should appear in the finished document. (Obj. 2)

1. Steven Maxey is to rent Apartment B-3 at 983 Eighth Place in Philadelphia, Pennsylvania for a period of one year beginning March 1, 19– at a monthly rent of $475.00. He has a cat. His rent includes utilities. ______________________

____

2. Fred and Samantha Wright are to rent Apartment 7 at 10 First Place in Philadelphia, Pennsylvania, starting on November 1, 19–. They have no pets, and will pay $625.00 per month including utilities. ______________________

____

3. William Wilbert is to pay $400 per month for a one-bedroom apartment at 307-D Shannon Chase, in Hempstead, New York. William is to pay for utilities himself. He will move in on July 1, 19–. His dog, Albert, will live with him. ______________________________

____

The following paragraphs contain the lease parts that are available for assembly.

File Name: LEASE BEGIN

APARTMENT LEASE

This lease agreement is made between AV APARTMENTS, LTD., hereinafter known as the landlord, and &tenant&, hereinafter known as tenant.

Landlord agrees to lease to tenant for a period of one year the apartment known as &address&. Tenancy is to begin on &date&. Tenant agrees to pay rent of &rent& per month, payable in advance. Tenant agrees to use the property as a personal residence only. No business may be conducted from the premises. Tenant agrees to pay first and last month's rent prior to occupying the premises.

File Name: PET

Tenant agrees to pay a security deposit of $400.00 prior to occupancy. A domesticated dog or cat weighing no more than 20 pounds may be kept on the premises as a pet so long as pet does not become a nuisance. Upon complaint by two or more neighbors, any such pet must be removed. Tenant agrees to be responsible for all deterioration or destruction of the premises caused by negligence or misuse. The amount of security deposit shall not limit the amount of tenant's liability.

File Name: NO PET

Tenant agrees to pay a security deposit of $200.00 prior to occupancy and agrees that no animals of any kind will be kept on the premises. Tenant agrees to be responsible for all deterioration or destruction of the premises caused by negligence or misuse. The amount of security deposit shall not limit the amount of tenant's liability.

File Name: UTILITIES

The monthly rent includes electricity, water, and gas. Tenant agrees to install and use no appliances other than normal household appliances unless express arrangements can be made in advance with landlord.

File Name: NO UTILITIES

The cost of utilities is not included in the monthly rent. Tenant shall establish own account with supplier of each utility.

File Name: LEASE END

This lease will be renewed automatically unless written notice of termination is given by either party at least 30 days before the end of the lease period. Landlord may change the amount of monthly rent for a renewal term by giving written notice at least 30 days before the end of the current lease period.

In case of breach of this agreement by tenant, tenant agrees to pay all legal expenses incurred by landlord in protecting landlord's rights under this agreement. All provisions of this agreement are to be governed by the laws of the state in which the premises are located.

______________________________ ____________
Tenant Date

______________________________ ____________
Landlord Date

COMPUTER EXERCISE

In this Computer Exercise, you will use the lease parts and situations given in the preceding Completion exercise.

1. Enter and save each of the lease parts as a separate file on disk.
2. Assemble and print leases for each of the three situations. Follow these steps for each lease:
   a. Erase any text that may be in the computer's memory.
   b. Load the *LEASE BEGIN* file from disk. Make sure the cursor is at the end of the file and press RETURN.
   c. Load all other files to be included in the lease.
3. Use the find and replace function to find the variable items (those enclosed in ampersands) and change them to the appropriate data. Refer to Lesson 23 if necessary to review the steps for finding and replacing.
4. Make any other necessary changes so that the wording of each lease matches the stated terms of the situation.
5. Save each assembled document to disk.
6. Print each assembled document.

25. Producing a Memorandum

OBJECTIVES:

1. Describe the format of a memorandum.
2. Explain how a glossary may be used to simplify the entry of commonly used words and phrases.
3. Tell how to use a glossary, and enter and print a memorandum.

Memorandums are written communications that are usually used between persons working in the same business. A memorandum's form is simpler than the form of a letter. Therefore, memorandums are easier to produce.

FORMAT OF A MEMORANDUM

Memorandums may be printed on either plain paper or preprinted forms. The format is almost the same on both kinds of paper. The following paragraphs describe the format of a memorandum.

Order of Parts

A typical memorandum has a four-line heading. The heading gives the name of the recipient, the name of the writer, the date, and the subject. If a preprinted form is being used, the words *TO:*, *FROM:*, *DATE:*, and *SUBJECT:* appear on the form as shown in Figure 25.1. If you are using plain paper, you arrange the headings in the same way.

```
                    INTEROFFICE COMMUNICATION

     TO:    Marvin Maxey  <------------ Indent 5 spaces

   FROM:    Helen Bunch  <------------- Indent 3 spaces

   DATE:    March 25, 19--  <---------- Indent 3 spaces

SUBJECT:    April 1 Bid Opening  <----- Left Margin
```

Figure 25.1 Headings of a Memorandum

After the headings, the body or message of the memorandum is printed. Standard letter format is used for the body. Usually paragraphs are not indented. The diskette notation is entered below the body. For an example of a completed memorandum, see Figure 25.2.

```
                        INTEROFFICE COMMUNICATION

     TO:   Marvin Maxey

   FROM:   Helen Bunch

   DATE:   March 25, 19--

SUBJECT:   April 1 Bid Opening


Please plan to attend the April 1 bid opening on the construction
of our new Raleigh facility.  Please meet Frank Moon and me in
the Board Conference Room at 1:30 p.m.

We are expecting bids from at least three companies, most likely
Artford Construction Company, Abeles and Associates, and RCP
Limited.  Please have your files on these three companies with
you for the opening.

sr:C212
```

Figure 25.2 Interoffice Memorandum

Margins

The top margin of a memorandum should be 1 1/2 inches. If the standard of 6 lines per inch is used, this gives a top margin of 9 lines. Side margins should be 1 inch. If the memorandum is printed at 10 CPI, the left margin setting is 10 and the right margin is 75. If the memorandum is printed at 12 CPI, the settings are 12 and 90.

Spacing

The headings of a memorandum are double-spaced. Between the headings and the body, there is a triple space. The paragraphs of the body are single-spaced, with a double space between paragraphs. There is a double space between the end of the body and the diskette notation.

USING A GLOSSARY

Apple Writer allows you to create a glossary to simplify the entry of commonly used words and phrases. To do this, you assign words and phrases to various keys. Then, by entering *[G]* (for glossary) followed by the assigned key, the entire word or phrase is inserted in the document. Suppose, for example, that Helen Bunch writes a lot of memorandums. So that you do not have to type her name repeatedly, you decide to set up a glossary entry. You assign Ms. Bunch's name to the *b* key. Then whenever you enter *[G]b*, her name is inserted into the text at the cursor.

Setting Up a Glossary

Each word or phrase you enter into a glossary is called a definition. Each definition is assigned to a key on the keyboard. Any key except the question mark key (?) and asterisk key (*) may be assigned a definition. Uppercase and lowercase letters are considered to be separate keys. Therefore, you could assign one definition to *A* and another to *a*. A glossary may be set up on a temporary or permanent basis.

SETTING UP A TEMPORARY GLOSSARY. Glossary definitions created during entry of text are temporary. That is, when the computer is turned off they will be lost. To set up a temporary definition, enter *[G]*. The prompt *[G]lossary(?=Define/*=Purge):* appears on the screen. Key a question mark, but do not press RETURN. Another prompt, *Enter new definition:*, appears. Now strike the key to which the definition will be assigned, and follow it immediately with the definition itself. Still using the example of Helen Bunch's name, you would key *bHelen Bunch.* Then press RETURN. To enter another definition, you repeat the entire process. To delete all glossary definitions from the computer's memory, enter *[G]** (the glossary purge command).

SETTING UP A PERMANENT GLOSSARY. Many times it is preferable to have a glossary that can be loaded from disk any time it is needed. This solves the problem of losing definitions when the computer is turned off. To set up a permanent glossary, you enter the definitions just as you would any text file. First, clear the computer's memory with the *[N]* command. (Make sure you have saved any important text before doing this.) Then enter the keys and definitions. It is wise to use a key that has a relationship to the definition. For example, you might enter the following:

bHelen Bunch
rregional managers
RRancho Grande Estates

After the glossary definitions are entered, simply save the file just as you would any text file by using the *[S]* command. Make up a file name that is easy to remember. It may be reasonable to set up a separate glossary file for each writer or for each subject area about which documents are produced. Including the word *GLOSSARY* in the file name will make it easy to remember what is contained in the file.

Before you can use the glossary file, you must load it into the computer's memory. Do this by entering *[Q]* for the Additional Functions Menu. Then enter Option 5 (*Load [G]lossary File*). When prompted, enter the glossary's file name. You can then use the glossary.

Glossary Limitations

There are some limitations that must be observed in setting up a glossary. As already mentioned, definitions may not be assigned to the question mark key and asterisk key. The total length of all keys and definitions in one glossary cannot exceed 2,048 characters. In a temporary glossary, no individual definition can exceed 128 characters. In a permanent glossary, an individual definition can be up to 2,048 characters long. If this is the case, however, there can only be one definition because it takes all the available space.

LESSON 25 EXERCISE Name ______________________ Date ____________

TRUE/FALSE

Each of the following statements is either true or false. Indicate your choice in the Answers column by circling T for a true statement or F for a false statement.

		Answers	
1.	Memorandums are usually used for correspondence between persons in different businesses (Obj. 1)	1. T	F
2.	Because memorandums have varying formats, they are always printed on plain paper (Obj. 1)	2. T	F
3.	As with a letter, the date is the first item to be printed on a memorandum (Obj. 1)	3. T	F
4.	The heading of a memorandum contains the name of the addressee, the name of the writer, the date, and the subject (Obj. 1)	4. T	F
5.	The top margin of a memorandum is 2 inches (Obj. 1)	5. T	F
6.	The left margin of a memorandum is 1 inch (Obj. 1)	6. T	F
7.	The right margin of a memorandum is 1 1/2 inches (Obj. 1)	7. T	F
8.	The body of a memorandum is single-spaced except between the paragraphs (Obj. 1)	8. T	F
9.	*Apple Writer*'s glossary feature automatically sets the margins for the proper memorandum format (Obj. 2)	9. T	F
10.	Glossary entries may be either temporary or permanent (Obj. 2)	10. T	F
11.	The use of a glossary can reduce the time required for the entry of many documents (Obj. 2)	11. T	F
12.	A glossary item is selected for entry into text by entering *[G]* followed by the key to which the item has been assigned (Obj. 2)	12. T	F
13.	Only one glossary can exist on the disk at any time; that is, when you save a new glossary, the old one is replaced (Obj. 2)	13. T	F
14.	A glossary definition may be any length (Obj. 2)	14. T	F

COMPLETION

Assume that you want to create a permanent medical glossary that contains the following definitions:

Key	Definition
c	cardiovascular system
a	arterial deposits
p	target pulse rate
D	M. E. McBrayer, M.D.
t	coronary thrombosis
s	cerebrovascular accident

On the lines below, write everything you will key to enter this glossary and save it on the disk. Use a file name of *HEART GLOSSARY* to save the glossary. (Obj. 2)

____

____

____

____

____

____

____

____

COMPUTER EXERCISE

In this Computer Exercise, you will enter and save a glossary. You will then use it to prepare a memorandum.

1. Enter the medical glossary from the preceding Completion section. Save it on diskette under the name *HEART GLOSSARY.*
2. Clear the computer's memory by using the *[N]* command.
3. Load the glossary that you entered in Step 1. (This glossary for learning purposes is rather short. Most actual glossaries would be longer.)
4. Enter, save, and print the following memorandum. The letters in parentheses are the glossary keys to use. This is done to help you remember to use the glossary instead of keying the entire term. Remember to use the correct memorandum format.

TO: H.R. Hanks FROM: (D) DATE: May 25, 19-- SUBJECT: Lunch Bunch Talk (Paragraph) Thanks for inviting me to address the hospital's Lunch Bunch Bonus for Business People on Thursday, June 27 at 12:30 p.m. I gladly accept your invitation. (Paragraph) The tentative name of my talk is "Eat and Run for your Heart." I will discuss the (c) in general and its role in good health. Much emphasis will be placed on the lessening of the risk of (t) and (s) if (a) are reduced through a proper program. I will outline the steps to developing a good recreation program, including the setting and use of a (p) as the best guide to the proper amount of exercise. (Paragraph) If you have any further suggestions on the topic, please let me know.

26. Introduction to WPL

OBJECTIVES:

1. Describe Word Processing Language.
2. Explain how to enter and save an address file.
3. Explain how to enter and save a Word Processing Language program.
4. Describe the procedure for running a Word Processing Language program.

You have learned about many important features of *Apple Writer* that make it a powerful word processor. One of the most important functions of any word processor, however, is the ability to create a file of information that can be used over and over. Such a file can be a list of frequently used names and addresses. Or it can be a form letter on file that is mailed to all the names and addresses in an address file.

WHAT IS WPL?

WPL, which stands for Word Processing Language, is a feature of *Apple Writer* that enables you to use automated word processing. WPL programs can be written to perform text editing and printing commands automatically. Because WPL is a type of computer programming language, it is beyond the scope of this text to explain how to write a WPL program. However, if after completing Lessons 26-29 you desire additional information about WPL, you can consult the WPL section of your *Apple Writer* manual. You will find that you are already familiar with many of the commands in the language because it uses control characters that were introduced earlier in this text.

CREATING AN ADDRESS FILE

Creating an address file is an easy process. After loading *Apple Writer* and clearing memory, simply enter each name and address that you want on file. Press RETURN after each line as shown in Figure 26.1. Key the less than (<) symbol and greater than (>) symbol immediately before each name and leave no space between the two symbols. Note also that there is no space following the > symbol, and there is no blank line between the city address and next name.

```
<>Mr. Kenneth M. Ellak
4288 Lago Circle
Lakeland, FL 33801-1217
<>Mr. Alfred Camps
7445 Stevens Creek Boulevard
Melbourne, FL 32905-6103
<>Miss Mary M. Malcolm
1118 Star Circle, Apt. 7
Naples, FL 33940-5422
```

Figure 26.1 Name and Address File

Before entering the names and addresses in the address file, you should determine some order in which to enter the information. You may choose alphabetic order using last names or numeric order using zip codes. This makes locating names and addresses in a large address file much easier.

Once you have entered all the names and addresses, you can save the file with an appropriate file name.

USING A WPL FILE

After you have created the address file, each of the names in the file must be assigned a number in consecutive order. You could have done this while entering the information. However, an easier way, especially if there are many names in the file, is to use the WPL program shown in Figure 26.2.

```
        PSX 1
        NY
        L filename,D1
        B
LOOP    F/<>/<(X)>/
        Y?
        PGO FOUND
        PGO QUIT
FOUND   PSX +1
        PGO LOOP
QUIT    S filename,D1
```

Figure 26.2 WPL NUMBER Program

When the program in Figure 26.2 is entered and saved, it can be run to automatically assign numbers consecutively to all of the names. Numbering of the names is required in order for another WPL program (discussed in Lesson 28) to use the names and addresses in producing form letters. When you enter the program in Figure 26.2, take care to enter it exactly as it appears, including spaces. You may enter the program in either uppercase or lowercase letters. Replace the word *FILENAME* in the third and last lines with the name that you used to save the address file. Enter the words *LOOP*, *FOUND*, and *QUIT* at the left margin. Indent the other lines.

After the program has been entered and saved, it should be run. To run a WPL file, enter *[P]*. In response to the *[P]rint/Program:* prompt, enter *DO NUMBER,D1* (assuming that the *NUMBER* program and address file are both loaded in Drive 1). As the program runs, you can watch the numbering process on the screen.

LESSON 26 EXERCISE Name ______________________ Date ____________

TRUE/FALSE

Each of the following statements is either true or false. Indicate your choice in the Answers column by circling T for a true statement or F for a false statement.

		Answers		
1.	WPL is a type of computer programming language (Obj. 1)	1.	T	F
2.	When an address file is entered, the < and > symbols are required immediately before the first line of the address (Obj. 2)	2.	T	F
3.	You enter a space between the < and > symbols (Obj. 2)	3.	T	F
4.	RETURN should be pressed after the person's name, the street address, and the city address (Obj. 2)	4.	T	F
5.	A blank line should be left after each address; that is, you press RETURN twice after each city address (Obj. 2)	5.	T	F
6.	An address file should be created in a certain order to help in locating addresses in the file (Obj. 2)	6.	T	F
7.	A file containing names and addresses is saved using the [S]ave function (Obj. 2)	7.	T	F
8.	In an address file that will be used to produce form letters, a number must be assigned to each name (Obj. 2)..	8.	T	F
9.	To assign a number to each name in an address file, you can use a WPL program or you can enter the number while creating the address file (Obj. 2)	9.	T	F
10.	To run a WPL program, enter *[P]* followed by the word *DO* and the name of the WPL program file (Obj. 4)	10.	T	F

COMPUTER EXERCISE

To complete this Computer Exercise, load *Apple Writer* and clear memory. Then follow the steps below:

1. Enter the names and addresses in Figure 26.1. Create two additional names and addresses and enter them also. Remember to arrange the addresses in alphabetic or zip code order.
2. Save the address file.
3. Clear memory. Then enter the WPL program in Figure 26.2. Remember to replace the word *FILENAME* in the third and last lines with the name you assigned to the file in Step 2.
4. Save the WPL file using *NUMBER* as the file name.
5. Run the WPL file by entering *[P]*. In response to the *[P]rint/Program:* prompt, enter DO NUMBER,D1 (assuming the file is on a diskette in Drive 1). Observe on the screen the numbers being added between the < and > symbols.
6. After the WPL program is finished, clear memory. Load and print the address file.

27. Producing Mailing Labels Using WPL

OBJECTIVES:

1. Explain how a mailing label is used.
2. Describe N-up mailing labels.
3. Explain how to enter and save a WPL mailing label program.
4. Explain the procedure for printing a set of mailing labels.

In Lesson 26 you learned how to enter and save an address file. After an address file has been created, it can be used repeatedly for printing continuous-form mailing labels. Mailing labels save much time when large volumes of written correspondence are to be mailed.

TYPES OF MAILING LABELS

When mailing labels are printed using either word processing or data processing equipment, continuous-form mailing labels are used that are similar to the ones illustrated in Figure 27.1. Note that the backing has the tractor-feed holes along the left and right edges of the paper that are necessary for guiding the labels through the printer in the same way as the continuous-form paper you have been using. After the labels have been printed, they are removed manually from the backing paper and applied to the envelopes.

Mailing Label Sizes

Mailing labels are available in a variety of sizes. The dimensions most typically used are 4 1/2 inches by 15/16 inches. This size allows room for five horizontal lines to be printed on each label. A typical business address uses one line each for the person's name, title, company, and street address, and one line for the city, state, and zip code. Labels used for personal correspondence require room for only three-line addresses since titles and company names are usually not included.

Figure 27.1 Continuous-Form Mailing Labels

N-Up Mailing Labels

Mailing labels can be purchased in one continuous strip, or they can be purchased with two, three, or four labels placed horizontally as in Figure 27.2. Mailing labels are also referred to as N-up labels. The N refers to the number of labels placed horizontally that are available for printing. For example, the labels in Figure 27.2 are called 4-up labels since there are four labels placed horizontally.

The reason for purchasing 2-, 3-, or 4-up labels is to obtain a faster printing speed. Most printers can print 1,000 labels, for example, faster using 4-up labels than 1-up labels since the print head moves faster horizontally than the tractor feed can move the labels up. In this lesson you will work with 1-up labels.

Figure 27.2 4-Up Continuous-Form Mailing Labels

PRINTING MAILING LABELS

A WPL program will be used later in the Computer Exercise to print the mailing labels from the address file you created in Lesson 26. The program is listed in Figure 27.3. Once this program has been entered and saved, it can be run to print labels from any file of addresses. The file name of the address file you created in Lesson 26 should be entered on the fifth line instead of the word *FILENAME*. The *D1* after the file name assumes that you will be using Drive 1. Save the program using the name *LABELS*. Before running the program you must determine how many lines will be needed for each address and select the appropriate size of continuous-form mailing labels.

```
START    PSX 1
         NY
         PND
LOOP     NY
         L filename,d1/<(X)>/</N
         PGO FOUND
         PGO QUIT
FOUND    PNP
         PSX +1
         PGO LOOP
QUIT     PIN       Done at address #(X)   (press RETURN)
```

Figure 27.3 WPL LABELS Program

The Print/Program Commands menu is used to determine the print format for the mailing labels. To do this, display the Print/Program Commands menu and enter the following trial settings:

LM = 5
RM = 100
TM = 0
BM = 0
LI = 0
SP = 0

A left margin (LM) of 5 leaves enough space for the print head to start printing on the label and not on the backing. The right margin (RM) can be set at any value as long as enough space is provided for the longest line of each address to print on a label. The top margin (TM) is set to 0 so that at least one blank line is left between the bottom of one label and the top of the next. The bottom margin (BM) should always be set to 0 for printing labels. A line interval (LI) of 0 is used since addresses are generally printed with no blank lines. Single page (SP) is set to 0 since you are using continuous-form mailing labels. Note: The use of these settings may cause your labels to be printed with a one-space indention on the first line of the address. This cannot be avoided.

Before loading the continuous-form mailing labels into the printer, you should enter the settings given above and print a trial run on regular paper. To do this, check to see that there is paper in the printer and then enter *DO LABELS* in response to the *[P]rint/ Program:* prompt. This assumes that the *LABELS* program and your address file are both saved on the same diskette and that the diskette is loaded in Drive 1.

Stop the printer by striking the ESC key after five or six labels have been printed. Remove the paper from the printer and lay it over the mailing labels by aligning the tractor-feed holes. By holding both pieces of paper up to the light you should be able to determine if your print values need to be corrected. Usually only the left margin and the top margin need to be corrected. Either increase or decrease the left margin setting to obtain the proper margins on the labels. Increase the top margin setting if more blank lines need to be left between labels. Because mailing labels are expensive, print as many trial runs as necessary before loading the mailing labels into the printer and printing the final run. After the correct format settings have been entered, save them in a Print/Program Value File as *LABELS*.

```
June 26, 19--



(ADDRESS)

Dear (TITLE) (LNAME)

Thank you for your recent order.  It has been
processed and sent to our shipping department.
You can expect to receive shipment within the
next thirty days.  If you do not receive
shipment during this time, please notify us
immediately.

Enclosed is our latest catalog.  We think you
will find that we have the best merchandise at
the best prices.  Your patronage is always
appreciated.

Sincerely



Jon S. Covington, Manager
Order Processing

jm:OP152

Enclosure
.FF
```

Figure 28.1 Form Letter

```
<>Mr.@F@Tim@M@M.@L@Carey
Director, Administrative Services
Workforce, Inc.
5 Corporation Lane
Washington, DC 20009-6633
<>Mrs.@F@Ora@M@W.@L@Godwin
Director, Purchasing Department
Southeastern Printing Supplies
3889 Neptune Drive
Independence, MO 64055-7121
<>Mr.@F@Mark@M@M.@L@Matthews
Office Manager
Yellow Sun Manufacturing, Inc.
489 Sansome
Arlington, VA 22202-2378
```

Figure 28.2 Address File

Each name in the address file is entered with the less than (<) and greater than (>) symbols on the first line as you learned in Lesson 26. After the title punctuation mark, you must enter the @ symbol, the capital letter *F*, and another @ symbol. Then enter the person's first name. Immediately after the first name, enter *@M@*. Then enter the person's middle initial. Enter *@L@* immediately after the period after the person's middle initial. Then enter the person's last name. The codes tell the computer how to determine the parts of the person's name. Observe that there are no blank spaces in the name line.

The *NUMBER* file you created in Lesson 26 is then run to assign numbers consecutively to all of the addresses. You must do this before you attempt to print the form letters.

WPL FORM LETTER PROGRAM

The WPL program to produce form letters is presented in Figure 28.3. When the program is run, it takes the first address from the address file and merges it with the form letter where the *(ADDRESS)* marker is located. It then removes the title from the name line and inserts it at the *(TITLE)* marker, and removes the person's last name and inserts it at the *(LNAME)* marker. Then the computer prints the letter. Observe in Figure 28.1 that a form feed (*.FF*) must always be entered at the end of a form letter so the paper will advance before the next letter is printed.

This program can also be used to print a person's first name in the salutation. To do this, you remove the markers *(TITLE)* and *(LNAME)* from the form letter and insert *(FNAME)* after *Dear*.

In the Computer Exercise, when you enter the WPL program in Figure 28.3 you must enter the name of your address file wherever *ADDRESS FILE NAME* appears. You must also enter the name of your letter file where *LETTER FILE NAME* appears. Proofread carefully to make sure that the WPL program is entered as it appears. Save the WPL program with the file name of *AUTOLETTER*.

Before printing the form letters, enter *[P]* and *?* to set the format values. If you are using single-sheet paper, SP must be set to 1. Then in response to the *[P]rint/Program:* prompt, enter *DO AUTOLETTER* and press RETURN. Each address appears briefly on the screen. The form letter replaces the address on the screen and the address is merged into the letter. The *(TITLE)* and *(LNAME)* markers are then replaced. The letter prints and a form feed occurs. The computer then selects the next address from the address file and repeats the process until all of the addresses have been used. The screen then displays *Done at address #5 (press RETURN)*. Press RETURN, and the Data Line reappears.

```
START    PSX 1
LOOP     NY
         L address file name,D1/<(X)>/</
         B
         S WORKFILE,D1
         NY
         L letter file name,D1
         B
         F/(ADDRESS)//
         Y?
         L address file name,D1/<(X)>/</N
         PGO FOUND
         PGO QUIT
FOUND    P INSERT TITLE FROM address file name,D1 INTO FORM LETTER
         PLS WORKFILE,D1/>/@/N=$A
         B
         F/(TITLE)/$A/A
         P INSERT FIRST NAME
         PLS WORKFILE,D1/@F@/@/N=$A
         B
         F/(FNAME)/$A/A
         P INSERT LAST NAME
         PLS WORKFILE,D1<@L@<><N=$A
         B
         F/(LNAME)/$A/A
         P DELETE MARKERS IN FORM LETTER
         B
         F/@F@/ /A
         B
         F/@M@/ /A
         B
         F/@L@/ /A
         PNP
         PSX +1
         PGO LOOP
QUIT     PIN    Done at address #(x)   (press RETURN)
```

Figure 28.3 WPL AUTOLETTER Program

LESSON 28 EXERCISE Name ______________________ Date __________

TRUE/FALSE

Each of the following statements is either true or false. Indicate your choice in the Answers column by circling T for a true statement or F for a false statement.

	Answers
1. A form letter is designed to be sent to only one person (Obj. 1)	1. **T** **F**
2. When a form letter is created, it usually contains a date, a specific person's name and address, and the salutation (Obj. 1)	2. **T** **F**
3. The WPL program looks for markers to determine where the letter address and salutation are to be placed (Obj. 1)	3. **T** **F**
4. Markers used in a form letter file must be spelled exactly the same in the WPL program (Obj. 1)	4. **T** **F**
5. An address file requires special formatting for the computer to determine a person's title, first name, middle initial, and last name (Obj. 2)	5. **T** **F**
6. When an address file is created to be used with a form letter, there should be no blank spaces in the name line (Obj. 2)	6. **T** **F**
7. The code *@L@* marks the beginning of the addressee's first name (Obj. 2)	7. **T** **F**
8. The *AUTOLETTER* file in Figure 28.3 should be entered exactly as it appears (Obj. 3)	8. **T** **F**
9. If single-sheet paper is to be used in producing form letters, the format value *SP* should be set to *0* (Obj. 4)	9. **T** **F**
10. You can use the *AUTOLETTER* program in Figure 28.3 to produce form letters that use a person's first name by deleting *(LNAME)* from the form letter and replacing it with *(FNAME)* (Obj. 4)	10. **T** **F**

COMPUTER EXERCISE

To complete this Computer Exercise, you will need to load *Apple Writer* and clear memory. Then follow the steps below as you use the computer:

1. Enter the form letter presented in Figure 28.1. Remember to enter a form feed (*.FF*) on a separate line immediately after *Enclosure.*
2. Save the letter using an appropriate file name.
3. Clear memory. Enter the WPL program presented in Figure 28.3. Replace *ADDRESS FILE NAME* with the name of the address file you created in Lesson 26. Replace *LETTER FILE NAME* with the name of the file you assigned in Step 2 above. Take care to enter the rest of the the WPL program exactly as it appears.
4. Save the WPL program as *AUTOLETTER.*
5. Clear memory. Load the address file you created in Lesson 26.
6. Delete the blank space and insert *@F@* before the first name. Delete the blank space and insert *@M@* immediately before the initial or middle name. Delete the blank space and insert *@L@* immediately before the last name. Repeat this procedure for each name in your address file.
7. Add two names and addresses to the file. Remember to include the name formatting codes that you inserted in Step 6 above.
8. Save the new version of the address file using *[S] =*.
9. Set appropriate print format values (remember to set SP to 1 if single-sheet paper is to be used). Press RETURN to return to the text screen.
10. Insert paper into the printer and enter *[P]*. In response to the *[P]rint/Program:* prompt, enter *DO AUTOLETTER.*

29. Producing a Customized Document Using WPL

OBJECTIVES:

1. Explain how a personalized form letter is used.
2. Explain how to enter and save a personalized form letter.
3. Explain the procedure for using a WPL program to print a personalized form letter.

In Lesson 26 you created an address file to be used for printing mailing labels and for merging with form letters. Usually an address file is created only if it is to be used repeatedly, such as a customer file or your own personal address file. Businesses, however, frequently receive inquiries that require a personalized form letter in response. In cases like these, address files would probably not be created.

ENTERING A PERSONALIZED FORM LETTER

A form letter and a WPL program can be created to enter personalized information from the keyboard rather than retrieving it from a file on the diskette. A form letter that is used to respond to an inquiry is presented in Figure 29.1.

As in Lesson 28, markers are entered in the form letter where variable information is to be entered. The current date will be entered at *(DATE)*, the addressee's title (such as *Ms.*, *Mr.*, or *Dr.*) and full name will be entered at *(NAME)*, the addressee's company title at *(TITLE)*, the company name at *(COMPANY)*, the street address at *(STREET)* and the city, state, and zip code at *(CSZ)*. For the *(SALUTATION)* marker, you can enter either the addressee's first name, nickname, or title and last name, whichever is appropriate. Observe that the *(SALUTATION)* marker is also included in the first paragraph. This personalizes the letter and makes it more friendly.

A form feed (.FF) is placed at the end of the letter. This causes the printer to eject the letter after it has been printed. You can create almost any form letter you desire based on this model as long as you put the markers into the program exactly as they are spelled in the letter. If you wish to make the form letter a personal letter, omit the job title and company name. The WPL program presented in Figure 29.2 can be used without modification.

```
(DATE)


(NAME)
(TITLE)
(COMPANY)
(STREET)
(CSZ)

Dear (SALUTATION):

Thank you for your letter asking for
information about our software products.  I am
enclosing our catalog which lists each
product, a description, and the price.
(SALUTATION), we believe that you will find we
have the software product you are looking for,
whether it is for home, school, or business.

Ordering information and an order form are on
page 67. Or you may use our toll-free number,
1-800-555-9130, if you wish faster service.

Sincerely,



Trudy W. Blake
Customer Service Department

jm:CS245

Enclosure
.FF
```

Figure 29.1 Personalized Form Letter

WPL FORM LETTER PROGRAM

The WPL program to create a customized form letter is presented in Figure 29.2. This program should be entered exactly as it appears except that in the fifth line you replace *LETTER FILE NAME* with the file name you assigned to the letter. The *D1* after the file name assumes that the letter file is loaded in Drive 1. Save this form letter program with a file name of *RESPONSE*.

```
START    PSX 0
LOOP     NY
         PND
         PSX +1
         L        letter file name,D1
         PIN      ENTER CURRENT DATE:=$A
         F/(DATE)/$A/A
         PIN      ENTER FULL NAME:=$A
         F/(NAME)/$A/A
         PIN      ENTER PERSON'S TITLE:=$A
         F/(TITLE)/$A/A
         PIN      ENTER COMPANY NAME:=$A
         F/(COMPANY)/$A/A
         PIN      ENTER STREET ADDRESS:=$A
         F/(STREET)/$A/A
         PIN      ENTER CITY, STATE, ZIP:=$A
         F/(CSZ)/$A/A
         PIN      ENTER SALUTATION:=$A
         F/(SALUTATION)/$A/A
         PPR
         PIN PREPARE PRINTER; THEN PRESS RETURN
         PYD
         PNP
         NY
         PIN      CONTINUE?:=$A
         PCS/$A/Y/
         PGO LOOP
         PCS/$A/y/
         PGO LOOP
QUIT     PYD
         NY
         PIN (X) LETTERS PRINTED (press RETURN)
         QT
```

Figure 29.2 WPL Form Letter Program

RUNNING THE WPL RESPONSE PROGRAM

To run the *RESPONSE* program, enter *[P]*. In response to the *[P]rint/Program:* prompt, enter *DO RESPONSE*. Memory is erased and questions appear on your screen one at a time. Enter the required information as it is requested. If you make an error while keying the information but before pressing RETURN, you can use the backspace key to correct the mistake. If you discover you have keyed incorrect information after you have pressed RETURN, you must strike the ESC key to exit from the WPL program. To restart the program, enter *[P]* and *DO RESPONSE* again.

The screen displays *CONTINUE?* after each letter is printed. If you wish to continue, enter either *y* or *Y* (for yes). The series of questions will be repeated and the next letter will be printed. When you respond with either *n* or *N* (for no) to the *CONTINUE?* question, the screen displays *X LETTERS PRINTED (PRESS RETURN).* (*X* is replaced with the number of letters that were printed.) After pressing RETURN, you will be ready to begin your next job.

There are other types of documents that can be created using this method. Examples are apartment leases, invoices, memorandums, and contracts. Whenever a document is to be used repeatedly with only minor changes, a WPL program can be created to print the document.

LESSON 29 EXERCISE Name ______________________ Date __________

TRUE/FALSE

Each of the following statements is either true or false. Indicate your choice in the Answers column by circling T for a true statement or F for a false statement.

	Answers		
1. The basic content of personalized form letters is always different from one letter to the next (Obj. 1)	1.	T	F
2. A personalized form letter usually contains a date marker (Obj. 1)	2.	T	F
3. The same marker may be used only once in a form letter (Obj. 2)	3.	T	F
4. A form feed (*.FF*) should be entered as the first line in a form letter (Obj. 2)	4.	T	F
5. If an address file is not used in a WPL program, variable information must be entered from the keyboard (Obj. 3)	5.	T	F
6. If you make an error after pressing RETURN in responding to a WPL question, you use the backspace key to correct the error (Obj. 3)	6.	T	F
7. A WPL program can be interrupted by striking the ESC key (Obj. 3)	7.	T	F
8. Generally any kind of repetitive document is suitable for use with a WPL program if it requires variable information to be entered (Obj. 3)	8.	T	F

COMPUTER EXERCISE

To complete this Computer Exercise, you will need to load *Apple Writer* and clear memory. Follow the steps below as you complete this exercise:

1. Enter the letter from Figure 29.1. Remember to include a form feed (*.FF*) at the end of the letter.
2. Save the letter with an appropriate file name.
3. Clear memory and enter the WPL program in Figure 29.2. In the fifth line replace *LETTER FILE NAME* with the file name you assigned in Step 2. If the letter file is to be loaded in Drive 2, change *D1* to *D2* after the file name.
4. Save the WPL program using the file name *RESPONSE.*
5. Prepare the printer and select appropriate format codes. If you are using single-sheet paper, *SP* should be set to 1.
6. Clear memory and enter *[P].* In response to the *[P]rint/Program:* prompt, enter *DO RESPONSE.* Use the information given below to respond to the prompts as they appear on the screen. Enter a current date for each letter.

Ms. Elizabeth P. Czernowski
President
DataCorp, Inc.
4899 Mercury Avenue
Falls Church, VA 22042-3332

Mr. Robert Gold
Director, Product Development
Nova Software Company
4 Cedar Wood Road
Syracuse, NY 13204-7175

Mr. Lawrence G. Hooker
Corporate Controller
Allied Manufacturing, Inc.
1224 Deacon Drive
Cleveland, OH 44125-3125

Mrs. Linda Vandenberg
Director, Financial Reports Division
Ramirez, Callihan, and Smith Consultants
844 Peachtree
Saginaw, MI 48603-8636

NAME ______________________ DATE ____________

30. Theory Test 3

In this Lesson you will test your knowledge of the concepts and procedures you have learned in Lessons 22 through 29.

TRUE/FALSE

Each of the following statements is either true or false. Indicate your choice in the Answers column by circling T for a true statement or F for a false statement. NOTE: The objective number in parentheses following each question refers to the lesson number and corresponding objective number. For example, Obj. 22-1 indicates that the question was discussed in Lesson 22 and refers to the first objective in that lesson.

	Answers
1. Merging allows the creation of a new document from two or more existing documents (Obj. 22-1)	1. T F
2. To merge two documents, they must both be saved on diskette (Obj. 22-1)	2. T F
3. *Apple Writer* provides a special command for merging one document with another (Obj. 22-3)	3. T F
4. A document from diskette may be placed at any desired point in the document in the computer's memory (Obj. 22-3)	4. T F
5. At least one of the two documents to be merged by *Apple Writer* must be stored on diskette (Obj. 22-3)	5. T F
6. Once a document has been created by merging, no additional text may be entered from the keyboard (Obj. 22-3)	6. T F
7. The find and replace feature of a word processor allows words or phrases to be changed to other words or phrases (Obj. 23-1)	7. T F
8. If automatic replacement is selected, all occurrences of the specified text will be found, and replacement will take place after verification of each occurrence by the operator (Obj. 23-1)	8. T F
9. Automatic find and replace could be appropriately used to correct the spelling of a word that had been consistently misspelled (Obj. 23-1)	9. T F
10. The find function cannot be used apart from the replace function (Obj. 23-2)	10. T F
11. The slash mark (/) is always used with *Apple Writer* to separate the text to be found and the text to use as a replacement (Obj. 23-2)	11. T F
12. A wild card character may be used to find text for which you may not know all the characters (Obj. 23-2)	12. T F

13. By searching for RETURN characters, you can easily skip over entire paragraphs of text (Obj. 23-2).................................... 13. **T** **F**

14. When a document is assembled, the user merges various standard paragraphs from memory (Obj. 24-1).................................... 14. **T** **F**

15. Since a will must be written especially for each individual, assembly with a word processor is not possible (Obj. 24-1) .... 15. **T** **F**

16. Different parts of text may be loaded from the disk and combined in memory to create a new document (Obj. 24-2) .... 16. **T** **F**

17. When a document is assembled from files on the disk, no text may be entered from the keyboard (Obj. 24-2).................................... 17. **T** **F**

18. The assembly of documents is a merging process (Obj. 24-2) .... 18. **T** **F**

19. Once a document is assembled in memory, it may be saved to disk and printed (Obj. 24-2) .... 19. **T** **F**

20. Memorandums are usually used for correspondence between persons in different businesses (Obj. 25-1).................................... 20. **T** **F**

21. As with a letter, the date is the first item to be printed on a memorandum (Obj. 25-1) .... 21. **T** **F**

22. The heading of a memorandum contains the name of the addressee, the name of the writer, the date, and the subject (Obj. 25-1).................. 22. **T** **F**

23. The top margin of a memorandum is 2 inches (Obj. 25-1) .... 23. **T** **F**

24. The left margin of a memorandum is 1 inch (Obj. 25-1) .... 24. **T** **F**

25. *Apple Writer*'s glossary feature automatically sets the margins for the proper memorandum format (Obj. 25-2).................................... 25. **T** **F**

26. A glossary item is selected for entry into text by entering *[G]* followed by the key to which the item has been assigned (Obj. 25-2) .... 26. **T** **F**

27. In entering an address file in WPL, the < and > symbols are required immediately before the first line of the address (Obj. 26-2) .... 27. **T** **F**

28. RETURN should be pressed after the person's name, the street address, and the city address (Obj. 26-2) .... 28. **T** **F**

29. A file containing names and addresses is saved using the [S]ave function (Obj. 26-2) .... 29. **T** **F**

30. In an address file that will be used to produce form letters, a number must be assigned to each name (Obj. 26-2).................................... 30. **T** **F**

31. To assign a number to each name in an address file, you can use a WPL program or you can enter the number while creating the address file (Obj. 26-2) .... 31. **T** **F**

32. To run a WPL program, enter *[P]* followed by the word *DO* and the name of the WPL program file (Obj. 26-4).................................... 32. **T** **F**

33. Mailing labels printed using word processing equipment are usually on continuous-form paper (Obj. 27-1) .... 33. **T** **F**

34. A typical business address contains four lines (Obj. 27-1).................. 34. **T** **F**

35. The N in N-up mailing labels refers to the number of mailing labels placed vertically (Obj. 27-2).. 35. **T** **F**

36. Any size mailing label can be used for printing an address (Obj. 27-4).... 36. **T** **F**

37. The Print/Program Commands menu is used to set the format values for printing mailing labels (Obj. 27-4).. 37. **T** **F**

38. A trial printing of the address file using regular paper should be completed before inserting continuous-form mailing labels in the printer (Obj. 27-4) 38. **T** **F**

39. When a form letter is created, it usually contains a date, a specific person's name and address, and the salutation (Obj. 28-1)........................ 39. **T** **F**

40. Markers used in a form letter file must be spelled exactly the same in the WPL program (Obj. 28-1).. 40. **T** **F**

41. An address file requires special formatting for the computer to determine a person's title, first name, middle initial, and last name (Obj. 28-2)........ 41. **T** **F**

42. When an address file is created to be used with a form letter, there should be no blank spaces in the name line (Obj. 28-2)........................ 42. **T** **F**

43. The code *@L@* marks the beginning of the addressee's first name (Obj. 28-2).. 43. **T** **F**

44. If single-sheet paper is to be used in producing form letters, the format value *SP* should be set to *0* (Obj. 28-4).. 44. **T** **F**

45. The basic content of personalized form letters is always different from one letter to the next (Obj. 29-1).. 45. **T** **F**

46. A personalized form letter usually contains a date marker (Obj. 29-1).... 46. **T** **F**

47. A form feed (*.FF*) should be entered as the first line in a form letter (Obj. 29-2).. 47. **T** **F**

48. If you make an error after pressing RETURN in responding to a WPL question, you use the backspace key to correct the error (Obj. 29-3)...... 48. **T** **F**

49. A WPL program can be interrupted by striking the ESC key (Obj. 29-3) 49. **T** **F**

50. Generally any kind of repetitive document is suitable for use with a WPL program if it requires variable information to be entered (Obj. 29-3)..... 50. **T** **F**

Glossary

[B]: control character that moves the cursor to the beginning of the file and sets the arrow on the Data Line to >

Backup copy: copy of files on diskette

Buffer: temporary storage space on diskette reserved for text

Character: any letter, number, symbol, or space that can be keyed on the keyboard

Computer program: group of instructions to the computer, often prerecorded on a diskette

Control character: letter that is struck while holding down the CTRL key

Cursor: flashing rectangle on the screen that moves as text is entered, always showing the position at which the next character entered will be displayed.

[D]: control character that changes the direction of the arrow on the Data Line

Data Line: a status line displayed at the top of the screen that shows constantly updated information about the text

Delimiter: a character used to separate print items from each other

Diskette: a device similar in appearance to a stereo record on which text is magnetically recorded; also referred to as a disk or a floppy disk.

Diskette catalog: list of files stored on a diskette

Document: information on paper

[E]: control character that moves the cursor to the end of the file and sets the arrow on the Data Line to <

Edit: change text

Embedded print commands: print commands that are placed in the text

[F]: control character used with *Apple Writer*'s find and replace function

File: text for a document stored on diskette

[G]: control character used with *Apple Writer*'s glossary function

Heading: title of a report that tells what the report is about

[I]: control character that moves the cursor to the tab positions set by using [T]

Initialization: a process that prepares the diskette to accept files

[K]: control character used to make a series of capital letters

[L]: control character used to load a file from diskette

Line interval: the number of blank lines between lines of print

Loading: process of reading text from a diskette and placing it into the computer's memory

Lock: protect a file on diskette so that it cannot be erased or permanently changed

Menu: list of functions the word processor can do

Merging: process of putting together one or more text files to create a new document

[N]: control character used to erase memory

[O]: control character used to view the DOS Commands menu

[P]?: control character used to view the Print/Program Commands menu

Powering down: turning off the different pieces of computer equipment

Powering up: turning on the different pieces of computer equipment

Prompt: message from a computer program telling the user what to do next.

[Q]: control character used to view the Additional Functions Menu

[R]: control character used to change from text-entry to replace mode

Report: a document that presents information in paragraph form

[S]: control character used to save a file on diskette

Save: copy a file from the computer's memory onto a diskette

Scrolling: a feature of *Apple Writer* by which text moves up the screen as it is entered and disappears, but remains in memory

Superscript: number raised slightly above the line that is used to indicate a footnote

[T]: control character used to set and clear tab stops

Text: groups of words

[W]: control character used to delete or insert a word

WPL: Word Processing Language—a feature of *Apple Writer* in which programs can be written to perform text-editing and printing commands automatically

Write-protect tab: small piece of special adhesive paper that prevents destruction of files on diskette

[X]: control character used to delete or insert a paragraph

[Z]: control character used to turn word wrap on or off